THE ANATOMY OF A
GOLF COURSE

THE ANATOMY OF A
GOLF COURSE

TOM DOAK

Lyons & Burford, Publishers

Printed in the United States of America

10 9 8 7 6 5 4 3 2

Library of Congress Cataloging-in-Publication Data
Doak, Tom.
The anatomy of a golf course / Tom Doak.
p.   cm.
Includes bibliographical references and index.
ISBN 1-55821-146-2
1. Golf courses—Design and construction.   I. Title.
GV975.D63   1992   92-6212
                                         CIP

CONTENTS

ACKNOWLEDGMENTS

Lou Gehrig said he considered himself the luckiest man on the face of the earth, but I wasn't around then. To be where I am today, making a good living at doing something I love—building golf courses—I've had to be more than lucky. I've had a lot of help.

Everything started with my dad, who let me start tagging along on his business conference/golf trips when I was ten or eleven years old. If those trips didn't turn me into a scratch golfer, they did introduce me to courses like Harbour Town, Pebble Beach, and Pinehurst No. 2, which were quite a change from the municipal course in Connecticut where I learned the game. In the process, I became fascinated with the differences between golf courses.

Next, I have to thank my faculty in the Landscape Architecture program at Cornell University, who didn't flinch when I told them I wanted to be a golf course architect; and especially a Cornell alumnus named William Frederick Dreer, who left an endowed scholarship for our department enabling me to spend a year studying the great golf courses of the British Isles, including a spell as a caddie on the Old Course at St. Andrews, and visits to 172 different golf courses all told. Ezra Cornell declared he "would found an institution where any man can pursue any study," and I'm living proof they still take that motto seriously on the shores of Cayuga Lake.

My travels didn't stop there, however, thanks to the staff and members of many private clubs in the United States and abroad who opened their arms to a college student requesting permission to study their golf courses. There are literally hundreds of people to whom I am indebted in this regard, including a few who took me into their homes, and who I still count among my closest friends—Bill Shean, Fred Muller, Andre Buckles, Johnny Stevens, Woody Millen, Walter Woods, and Richie Benaud, to name just a handful.

Those travels left me with a love of good golf courses, and a fair grasp of the principles of sound design; yet I never would have been able to make the leap from student to architect without the guidance of Pete and Alice Dye and their sons, Perry and P. B. After I had bugged them by constantly writing letters for a couple of years, they let me come to work for them, in the most menial capacity, on the construction of Long Cove Club in the summer of 1981. For four years afterward I followed along from Plum Creek to PGA West to Riverdale Dunes and Piping Rock, gradually becoming more involved in the construction of their courses, and occasionally getting to contribute my two cents worth to the final design. Of all the things I learned from Pete, the most important was just how much work was involved in getting a great golf course from the dream to the ground. That is one lesson I hope will come across clearly in this book.

While associated with the Dyes, I was also lucky enough to work with many talented people who are too often overlooked in their contributions to the success of golf courses—shapers like Scott Pool and Jim Urbina (who taught me how to run a bulldozer), construction managers like David Postlethwait and Lee Schmidt (both of whom are now golf architects in their own right), and Neal Iverson, who taught me the value of a well-designed irrigation system. When I took on my first solo project at High Pointe in Michigan, I was fortunate to be able to rely on my construction superintendent and "grass guru" Tom Mead. Tom made the concept of fescue fairways and greens in northern Michigan a reality and taught me most of what I know about the use and limitations of turfgrasses.

I must also thank all the well-known members of the golf community who offered their advice and encouragement. Fellow architects Ben Crenshaw, Geoffrey Cornish, Rees Jones, Tom Fazio, Tom Weiskopf, and Ron Whitten, the most qualified nonarchitect in the world, openly shared their ideas with me. The peerless golf course photographer Brian Morgan helped me enormously during my year overseas, and George Peper at GOLF Magazine allowed me to start writing about golf architecture while I waited for my real career to take off. Just by taking me seriously, all of these people made me that much more determined to succeed at my craft and repay their faith in me.

Ultimately, however, no golf architect can be successful without patrons who will commission him to work with their land. I must thank Larry and Danny Young at The Legends, David Smith at Wilderness Valley, and John Gorman at Harbour View for giving me outstanding opportunities to show what I can do. Doug Grove, Dave Richards, and Brian Morgan provided the references which led to those jobs. Most of all I must thank Don Hayden, the developer of High Pointe, who entrusted a 26-year-old rookie architect with a good budget and a beautiful piece of land, and then gave me the freedom to put years of theories into practice without having to defend my choices. I only wish the current management was as sympathetic to preserving those ideals.

As for this book itself, I must first thank Peter Burford, for his conviction in publishing a "serious" golf book without the mass-market appeal of the endless coffee-table golf course picture books. All of the golf-hole diagrams are the handiwork of my talented design associate Gil Hanse, whose patience for detail serves him well as a designer as well as an illustrator.

Several friends were kind enough to read through the

manuscript and make suggestions: Gil Hanse, Tom Mead, David Earl, Ben Crenshaw, and especially my wife, Dianna Johnson. Dianna not only helped me refine my ideas throughout the year the book was in the works, but also delivered our first son, Michael, in the meantime.

Finally, none of this would have been possible without the encouragement of my mom, Betty Burch Doak. She grew up on a farm in Missouri, which is where I think my love of the land came from. She was the one who taught me to write, since she had been an editor for the agricultural extension services at the University of Delaware and at Cornell University before she was a mom. Later, when I wanted to pursue golf architecture as a career, she obtained copies through interlibrary loan of the wonderful books on the subject written by Alister Mackenzie, George Thomas, and Robert Hunter, and made two copies of each—one for me, and one for herself to read. Of course, she would have been proud of anything I'd decided to do, but I am sure that it was one passage from Mackenzie's book that convinced her I was pursuing a noble profession: "One of the reasons why I, 'a medical man', decided to give up medicine and take to golf architecture was my firm conviction of the extraordinary influence on health of pleasurable excitement, especially when combined with fresh air and exercise."

I wish she had lived to see this book completed, because it probably would have benefitted from her editorial eye, but I will be satisfied if it inspires one more person to appreciate the beauties of golf courses the way my mom did.

FOREWORD

Tom Doak has received one of the finest educations of anyone in golf architecture. He won a scholarship from Cornell to travel abroad and study all the courses he could find. Not coincidentally, Robert Trent Jones, Sr., also attended Cornell and has made it possible for many other students to learn about golf in the same way. Tom's partner in golf design, Gilbert Hanse, won the same scholarship and has just collaborated on a new book, *Colt & Co.*, based on the life of England's great architect Harry Colt. These happy activities fueled the fire that inspired both these young men in their appreciation for golf architecture. So off they went to the

British Isles, disguised as modern-day Hugh Wilsons. Wouldn't it make perfect sense, they thought, to absorb the great and timeless works of the old masters, just as would any budding art student?

It amazes me how sound were the great architects. Each had his own interpretation, and each built a sense of character, naturalness, playability, and beauty wherever their "easel" took them. Each man had a unique style—brush strokes, if you will—making their finished courses all but unmistakable. Who with a well-tutored eye could not identify a Mackenzie bunker, a Ross green, a Thomas mound, or a Tillinghast hole? Their work bears the stamp of their personalities, beliefs, and opinions—the delicate blending of science and art that adds up to a pleasurable experience on the golf course. These are the qualities that elevate great courses above good ones.

I think every course worth playing retains some small element or spirit of the Old Course at St. Andrews. She is the original—*the* course that has survived and defended the spirit of the game against the advancement of technology and the efforts of a few cocky know-it-alls who are unwilling to learn her many fascinations. St. Andrews is a living testament to the canny Scots, who have always had the good sense to leave well enough alone and walk hand-in-hand with Nature. For five hundred years she has held the fascination of both duffer and expert, even with gigantic roller-coaster double greens, unseen bunkers, cross-fire holes, and a million small humps that kick this way and that. So much the better. It's for everyone to choose his own path to glory—or perdition.

In St. Andrews we have a course worthy of lifelong study for serious architecture students, to heed her call and absorb the soundness of her principles. Fertile minds such as those of J. L. Low, Horace Hutchinson, Dr. Alister Mackenzie, the great Bobby Jones all thought so. The course demands a new line or route with even the slightest change of wind angle. St. Andrews remains the ultimate thinking course, forcing players to accept the tenet that *Nature appears at random.*

It is up to the golf architect to present us with a thinking contest as well as a physical one. It is the rare course today that reflects the proper balance of these two important ingredients as the great courses do. It is not my lot to comment on individual design efforts these days. There is good reflective work being done by people who are not golf stars and do not get the credit they're due, as well as plain work by players or those otherwise at the top. This much is certain—we have to be careful that golf design does not evolve into a frenzied race to cut the ribbon on real-estate sales. Good golf demands more attention than that. Nature is too important to receive ill regard. Few endeavors place such heavy burdens on the consciences of those involved, whether developers or designers. If we are to preserve the integrity of golf as left to us by our thoughtful forefathers, it is up to all of us to carry on the true spirit of the game.

Tom Doak is a fellow "protectionist" and a *real* lover of the game. I am not alone in thinking he is a terrific writer. Among many other topics, his book is a look at building courses today, and what he has to say comes at an important juncture. I hope this book will inspire the best work in all of us. I like to think of this book as an update on the great architecture books of the past: *Scotland's Gift, Golf* by Charles Blair MacDonald, George C. Thomas' *Golf Architecture in America, The Architectural Side of Golf* by Tom Simpson and H. N. Wethered, and Dr. Alistair Mackenzie's *Golf Course Architecture.* How precious little they left us! In *The Anatomy of a Golf Course,* Tom Doak reaches the salient points vividly, with forceful quotes from those who have really mattered, and delightful descriptions of the why's and how's of fine golf architecture.

We have a faithful ally in him, and he will go far in this business, because he loves it for golf's sake.

BEN CRENSHAW, February, 1992

INTRODUCTION

"To learn golf architecture one must know golf itself, its companionships, its joys, its sorrows, its battles—one must play golf and love it."
— GEORGE THOMAS, Golf Architecture in America: Its Strategy and Construction, 1927.

Every golfer fancies himself to be a golf course architect. Just like the moviegoer or the museum visitor, we may not fully understand the creative process, but we know what we like. And the fact that golf courses are interactive—they are built to be played—gives the golfer special license to criticize.

Luckily for the golf architect, one of the perversities of the game is that while the good player tends to remember his misfortunes (and is therefore a tough critic), the average golfer accentuates the positive in remembering the course. Some modern courses, such as the notorious Stadium Course at PGA West, rely upon this phenomenon. Every hole is so difficult that whenever the golfer hits the ball squarely—as he is bound to do, somewhere over the course of 18 holes—the shot will clear such impressive obstacles that he will treasure it as one of the best shots of his life, and remember the course with pleasure, forgetting the other 140 strokes of the day.

Selective memory also helps to explain why every golfer holds his home course in high esteem, regardless of its merits. Both good players and bad have simply played their home course enough to have fond memories of each hole, whether those memories come from a single birdie or a wealth of successes.

There are, however, a few courses that transcend the golfer's limited perspective. On these courses, the beauty of the setting and the hazards of each hole inspire the golfer to play his best. At the same time, each hole is designed so that no matter where the golfer may find himself on his way to holing out, he is still "in the game." The golf course is only a medium which makes the game more interesting; it is not supposed to be an obstacle course, eliminating the player who trips up first. Given no chance to recover, the faltering golfer quickly loses interest in the game. To design courses that can be enjoyed even when you're playing badly, and that will stand the test of time, is the art of golf architecture.

The few courses around the world which are agreed to be the finest in the game are so different from the average course that it is impossible for someone who has never seen them to realize the potential of golf architecture: courses totally in harmony with the land, beautiful in their own workings, and functional for all levels of golfers.

While a golfer who has traveled extensively may appreciate good golf architecture, it is a far different thing to be good at it. To design a great course one must also possess the artistic ability to visualize a design in a given landscape, a familiarity with the land which comes only from spending time on it, and enough knowledge of golf construction and maintenance to realize one's ideas on the ground and guarantee their endurance.

While a great deal of attention has been devoted in recent years to picture books of the great courses, little has been written about the art of golf design, and the science of translating the design to the ground. Most successful architects have been too busy designing to sit down and explain what they're doing; a few are too competitive to reveal their secrets to the competition.

By contrast, during the so-called golden age of golf architecture in the 1920's, many of the leading designers wrote books on the subject, the few remaining copies of which are treasured by architects and collectors today. The four best were Dr. Alister Mackenzie's *Golf Architecture*, a short and philosophical look at the art of design; George Thomas's *Golf Architecture in America*, the most thorough how-to book on the subject to date; H. N. Wethered and Tom Simpson's *The Architectural Side of Golf*, featuring Simpson's wonderful freehand drawings; and Robert Hunter's *The Links*, a detailed analysis of golf and golf courses of the period on both sides of the Atlantic.

The wisdom of these old books is timeless, but the practice of golf architecture has changed dramatically since the most recent of them was published in 1929. Of the authors, only Tom Simpson lived long enough to see the widespread use of the bulldozer in golf course construction. Lord only knows what the colorful and gruff Mackenzie would have made of the lava flows of Mauna Kea, or the island-green 17th hole at the Tournament Players Club at Sawgrass. While I have little confidence that this book will make as good reading in the year 2065 as the aforementioned books do today, another good book on the subject is long overdue—one which brings us up to date on the science and practice of golf architecture, while still stressing the artistic aspects which those earlier architects instinctively understood.

I hope that reading this book will prompt golfers to pay critical attention to the art of golf architecture. Every art needs good criticism if it is to flourish, and it is peculiar that in a business involving such large expenditures so little objective criticism is to be found. Such criticism, once the province of the better golfers (particularly the Tour professionals), has disappeared now that anyone qualified to comment on the subject has thrown his hat in the ring as a designer in his own right. From architecture to autos to fashion, the "designer label" has become more coveted than the product itself. Name recognition has become the most important qualification for success in the modern business, and most who have achieved it are too busy with other pursuits to devote their time to the realization of "their designs." As a result, individual courses seldom receive the attention to detail which might make them true works of art.

Some of my readers, particularly those with competing ambitions in the world of golf architecture, will no doubt question my authority to complete this work at the age of 30. I actually think it's beneficial to say my piece now, before I have become entrenched in my own style of design and too busy building courses to write about it. I don't think it's a coincidence that many of our greatest courses, including the National Golf Links of America, Pine Valley, Merion, and Pebble Beach, were the first courses completed by their designers, when their ideas were fresh and they did not have to allocate time between ten simultaneous projects. I am also amused to note that Mackenzie and Simpson set pen to paper before their design careers took off, while George Thomas got bored with golf design after explaining it, and went back to his other consuming hobby of growing roses.

1

THE MODERN GOLF COURSE

"It is quite certain that, had the ground on which ordinary inland golf is played today been the only available ground for the purpose, the game would never have been invented at all."
—GARDEN G. SMITH, The World of Golf, 1898.

Golf architecture is an art deeply rooted in tradition; and all of the best architects have sought to uphold that tradition in their work. Golf architecture does not need to be "reinvented." The art simply continues to be polished by those who understand it best.

It is important that the student of architecture understands the forces of change constantly at work within the game, because as the playing of golf changes, so must the interpretation of every course which already exists. Indeed, the history of golf architecture is defined by changes in equipment, course conditioning, and playing technique, which have forced architects to alter the demands of their designs. Therefore the quickest way to understand golf architecture is to study what have been recognized as the best courses since the earliest time, and to see how they have stood up to the forces of change.

The courses which will most reward study separate themselves into three distinct eras of design: the British links of the 19th century; the classic designs of the worldwide golf boom from 1900–1930; and the post-1945 "modern era" of courses constructed with the aid of the bulldozer. It is not the purpose of this chapter to recount the history of golf architecture or to draw conclusions as to the best or most influential courses, although I will include a substantial list of courses worth study in the appendix. But each era of design contains its own special lessons, and no one's education in the art could be considered complete without having seen at least a few courses from each of the three eras.

LINKS COURSES

It must be admitted that much of the publicity given to so-called Scottish designs in America today is really lip service to a marketable tradition that few writers truly understand at all. Some architects believe that they are capable of embracing the collective wisdom of the British courses on a ten-day whirlwind tour of St. Andrews, Carnoustie, Muirfield, Troon, Turnberry, and Gleneagles. Others, being more honest, would admit that they don't care much for the links courses, but recognize the sales value of a "Scottish" label.

Yet to truly understand the enduring popularity of golf and the essentials of good golf courses, it is imperative to become familiar with the British links over which the game evolved five centuries ago. The importance of studying the links is summarized by two facts: These are the courses over which the game itself was invented, and they have endured despite tremendous changes in almost all other aspects of the game.

The links were not designed for golf; at least, not by the hand of man. Natural forces of tide and wind produced the endlessly undulating contours in the sand, and animals provided the seeds for swards of turf and the scrapes that became enlarged into the bunkers. The equipment and rules of golf were designed to deal with the challenges found on the links.

There is a tremendous variety of golf holes and golf courses in Britain because the links terrain itself varies so widely from town to town. Linksland can be generally described as sandy and undulating, but the undulations vary widely in scale and frequency over 150 acres, and more still from course to course. This variety remains a part of the golf courses, because the designers were powerless to make large-scale changes to the terrain to standardize their designs. Indeed, since the routings of the early courses evolved through general agreement of the locals during an era when travel between towns was difficult, there were no accepted standards of good golf architecture, even as to the number of holes on a course. The links of Leith consisted of 5 long holes arranged in a loop, while Prestwick had 12 which crisscrossed back and forth, and St. Andrews had 22 holes—11 out to a distant point, then players turned around and played the same holes in reverse order.[1]

The great variety of holes in Britain allows the student of the game to see all the possibilities of golf course design, and to identify the holes and concepts which provide interesting play, and those which do not.

---

[1]Dr. Mackenzie wrote in 1920, "I believe the real reason St. Andrews Old Course is infinitely superior to anything else is owing to the fact that it was constructed when no-one knew anything about the subject at all, and since then it has been considered too sacred to be touched. What a pity it is that the natural advantages of many seaside courses have been neutralised by bad designing and construction work."

For the American visitor to Britain, the other revelation is that the game can be so enjoyable in such harsh conditions. The sandy soil underlying the links makes for a very firm and fast playing surface, on which it is difficult to control the bounce of the ball after it lands. Therefore the contours of the approach to the green play a significant role in the final disposition of the shot. The turf conditions themselves are erratic, because value is placed on the affordability of the game rather than on the upkeep of the courses to "championship" standards. And the links are completely exposed to the vagaries of coastal winds, imposing another layer of difficulty upon the play.

To compensate for all these natural difficulties, the one common thread in the design of the links is that there is a certain amount of leeway built into the demands for each shot. There is almost never a long forced carry to be made from the tee, because it would be impossible with a 50-mile-per-hour gale blowing in the golfer's face. There is rarely a small green surrounded by hazards, because it would be impossible to hold with the same strong wind blowing from behind the golfer. And the fairways are seldom really narrow, except as prepared for an Open Championship, because a strong crosswind would make them almost impossible to find.

This latitude for difficult conditions has a tremendously important side effect: It gives the weaker player a built-in margin for error. This is in direct contrast to the typical modern American course, where every green is designed under the assumption that the golfer will have a perfect lie from which to play and that the target should therefore be sized to always separate the good shot from the bad.

Because the difficulty of the links is attributable as much to the presence of wind and firm ground as to their architectural hazards, their challenge has survived improvements in course maintenance and golfing equipment which have rendered other old courses defenseless.

THE CLASSIC PERIOD (1900–1930)

Most of the courses of the classic era, in contrast, attempt to preserve the traditional challenges of the Scottish game, on land chosen for the purpose, but with hardly the same natural advantages of wind and undulation the links enjoy. These classic courses may not individually possess the great variety of terrain found on some of the British and Irish links, yet, because the classic-period courses were built on so many different types of ground in so many different countries and climates, the collective variety of golf holes is perhaps unsurpassed.

I think it can safely be said that more outstanding golf architects were in practice during the period from 1900–1930 than in any period before or since, if not more than in the rest of history combined. In Britain there was the firm of Herbert Fowler and Tom Simpson, responsible for many of the finest courses on the continent of Europe, and their part-time associates Abercromby and Croome. There was also the firm of Harry S. Colt, Alister Mackenzie, and Charles Alison, who would eventually produce outstanding courses on all six habitable continents. In America, where Colt and Mackenzie also flourished, there were Charles Blair Macdonald and his understudies, Seth Raynor and Charles Banks; Donald Ross; A. W. Tillinghast; George C. Thomas, Jr.; and the many "amateur" architects, from George Crump at Pine Valley and Jack Neville at Pebble Beach to William and Henry Fownes at Oakmont, and Hugh Wilson at Merion along with his protege, William Flynn. Even though they were competitors, many of these men wrote books on the subject and freely exchanged ideas, best exemplified in the construction of Pine Valley, where Colt, Alison, Tillinghast, Thomas, and Wilson all made suggestions to Crump. With such cooperation, the art of golf architecture quickly grew until the economics of the 1930's halted new construction.

Alternatively, the classic period can be defined by improvements in golfing technology. It was just after the turn of the century that the Haskell ball replaced the gutty, allowing the average player another 20 to 40 yards with each shot. Immediately almost all of the well-known early courses, those most praised by good players for their challenge, became pushovers, and many were changed architecturally to restore the difficulty that the new equipment had taken away. The first courses attempting to counter the new technology were controversial, but today those same courses—Oakmont and Pine Valley—are our accepted classics.

At the tail end of the classic era, further developments in technology, from the replacement of hickory shafts with steel and the development of the sand wedge to advances in construction equipment, led designers to redefine the bounds of golf architecture once again.

THE MODERN PERIOD

After World War II, Robert Trent Jones came to the forefront of the design business with his redesign of Oakland Hills for the 1951 U. S. Open Championship, and later for his innumerable 7,000-yards-and-up layouts like Bellerive and Hazeltine National, both selected as U. S. Open sites. The tandem of Pete Dye and Jack Nicklaus briefly reversed the tide of long and difficult courses with their characterful, short, and precise Harbour Town Golf Links in 1969. Yet in the new construction boom of the 1980's, both men achieved greater fame in their work for designing longer and more difficult courses, such as the TPC at Sawgrass (Dye) and Castle Pines Golf Club (Nicklaus).

All these modern courses represent a huge break from the links and even from the classic era because of the technology available for golf course construction after World War II.

Large earth scrapers and tilt-blade bulldozers replaced the mules and drag pans with which the final contours had been painstakingly sculpted on earlier courses. No longer bound by the general designs of Mother Nature, the modern golf architect has been able to reshape the land to fit his own theories of design.

The downside of modern construction is that many of the subtle contours of the natural landscape which make older courses so interesting are lost during the mass grading of modern layouts, and there is never enough time in the construction schedule to replace them in all their detail. Even features which might have been the cornerstone of a unique natural golf hole are sometimes bulldozed out of existence to make room for an artificial hazard concocted from the architect's mind. From the standpoint of the construction companies, the *modus operandi* which my friend Scott Pool jokingly described as "rape it, shape it, and grass it" (referring to the land, of course) has become the norm. Meanwhile, human nature has induced architects to repeat the forms which have been well-received in the past; the variety of holes to be found on new courses is far less than on old courses, even though the technology to create new holes from scratch has increased a hundredfold.

The other pitfall of the *carte blanche* which modern architects are given is the natural temptation to overdo things, to try and make every hole as fancy and theatrical as possible. In the process, the natural variety which God gives to the world— that some parts of the ground are more undulating than others—does not extend to the finished golf course. On many modern courses, each hole is harder than the last, and by the time the golfer reaches the 18th he is exhausted and uninterested. Tom Fazio and Steve Wynn's ultraprivate Shadow Creek, in Las Vegas, is the rare example of a calculated approach, with a measure of restraint on some of the early holes, thanks to Wynn's understanding of the art of showmanship.

The modern era of design has not been a total loss; one great advantage of modern technology is that it is now possible to transform barren and unproductive sites into beautiful golf courses. In the past twenty years, golf courses have been reclaimed from strip mines, quarries, and sanitary landfills, becoming an asset to the community rather than a liability. In other locales, ideal land for golf is simply not available, and the developer and architect must rely on their imaginations and a healthy creative budget. Jack Nicklaus's Desert Highlands, which successfully introduced golf into the hostile desert landscape, is a fine example of the latter.

The unfortunate result of these rare successes has been to convince developers that good land is no longer a necessary component of a good course. As a result, not enough attention is paid to selecting the best piece of property where a choice is available. The future of the art of golf architecture is bleak if total workovers are the only projects attempted.

PROPERTY SELECTION

Golf architects have been closing sales for 100 years with the observation that "God intended this land to be a golf course,"[2] regardless of the natural advantages of a given property. Sales pitches notwithstanding, the fact remains that most great courses are first and foremost the product of beautiful pieces of ground.

One of the main reasons it is difficult to build a great course today is that few developers select property with golf as their first priority. Golf was invented on land ideal for the purpose; in the golden age of design, most clubs still had a wide choice of property to pursue their dream of a first-class course. Today, many courses are tied in with resort or residential develop-

[2]First credit for this sales pitch, according to Horace Hutchinson's *Fifty Years of Golf*, goes to one General Moncrieffe of St. Andrews, who upon being shown the sandhills which now comprise Royal North Devon Golf Club, pronounced that "Providence obviously designed this for a golf links."

ments with their own priorities of site selection. Most of the rest are developed by private or municipal sources on whatever land is owned by the developer, or on sites so poor they cannot be used for any other purpose and are therefore cheap to acquire: flood plains, landfills, buffer zones, barren ground, or whatever land is zoned correctly.[3] The developer also stands to reap a greater profit if he can make something out of nothing, or if his architect promises he can.

Nevertheless, there is economic incentive for selecting good property for golf. The prestige factor of an outstanding course translates directly into higher land values for the surrounding property, and higher membership fees or green fees for the golf course. The developer who understands these values and desires a golf course of real quality should bring a golf architect into the project as early as possible to ensure that in selecting property he has taken into account the special considerations of golf. Often, better land for golf may be found just down the road from the property a developer might consider ideal.

Until a few years ago, the main factors the developer and golf architect had to consider in evaluating property were acreage, topography, soil, and vegetation. Today a fifth factor must be included—the all-encompassing environmental considerations. These can be so complicated in modern practice that property should only be optioned after environmental factors are fully explored.

Acreage

The first consideration is to ensure that enough acreage is available on which to build the course; generally speaking, the more property that can be acquired for the purpose, the better. If more land is acquired than needed, the golf course developer may choose to develop it with other amenities or sell it at

[3]In both Europe and Japan, land deemed ideal for agricultural production cannot legally be developed, thus restricting golf courses to land poorly suited to the purpose.

a profit, since his golf course is sure to raise the property value of surrounding land.

A good course and practice facility will generally require a minimum of something near 150 acres, and even more if there are extensive wetlands or steep hills which cannot be fitted into the scheme of the course, or if the parcel is so oddly shaped that there is no room to get holes in and out of a narrow corner. Given less ground to work with, the golf architect will be forced to shoehorn his holes into the available acreage instead of tailoring them to the natural features of the property.

The smallest 18-hole course I have seen that could be considered outstanding is the East course at Merion in Philadelphia, on just 126 acres including the clubhouse and parking; there was generous acreage to work with originally, and the unused property was sold at a later date. It is the result of ideal topography that such restricted properties as Merion and Inverness yield a golf course of great variety from a routing of parallel holes—such enforced plans usually produce banal results. Moreover, in the modern era of high-volume play, such courses would not provide an adequate margin of safety for players without the plantings between holes which have matured in the 75 years since their construction.

A modest club with a small membership might squeeze 18 holes onto as little as 90 to 100 acres, by employing such design tricks as double fairways à la St. Andrews, or crossover holes à la Old Prestwick. Because of reduced safety margins, however, such features will restrict play once the course becomes popular and undermine its potential for success.

If a property holds golfing interest, but sufficient acreage for 18 holes cannot be secured, other types of courses can be considered: a regulation-length 9 holes, a "precision" or "executive" layout of less than full length, or a course consisting entirely of par-3 holes.

The 9-hole layout must be the first option considered, as golfers have always resisted courses which do not allow them to unleash their full strength with a driver, an inherent part of the thrill of the game. Moreover, 9 good holes are much better than 18 cramped ones. A really well-designed course should lose no interest the second time around, even in the same afternoon, as such great courses as Whitinsville, Massachusetts, or Royal Worlington & Newmarket, England, exemplify.

I have always envisioned that some properties unsuitable for a regulation-length course might make an exciting par-3 course; for example, land so abrupt that one could not secure visibility on long holes or flatten it into workable fairway lies. The holes on such a course would ideally be varied from a 60-yard pitch to the length of a full drive. Unfortunately, most of the short courses I have seen fall well short of this vision, perhaps because few developers with modest aspirations hire a golf architect with imagination and give him the license to design something worthwhile. From the economic perspective, another drawback of a par-3 course is that the high cost of proper putting-green construction makes it a relatively expensive proposition, considering the diminished expectation of revenue. Such courses would be ideal for an existing club with extra acreage, and might provide a venue for beginning players to become attached to the game.

If more than 18 holes are contemplated, the designer must consider how the courses will relate to one another. For public and resort projects, it has been found that if the courses are not of similar length and difficulty, the weaker course will be largely ignored; many courses, from Gleneagles to Doral, have done costly reconstruction to eliminate this "perception problem." Yet at private clubs, one championship-length course and a shorter second course are often a very popular combination: witness Winged Foot, Merion, Baltusrol, or even Augusta National, with its par-3 addition.

Topography

Aside from sufficient acreage, topography is the foremost quality of a good property. If it is ideal, a course can be laid out requiring almost no heavy construction, apart from shaping the greens, tees, and bunkers. A good topographic map, with a contour interval of 5 feet and scale of 200 feet to the inch, is essential for laying out the course; a contour interval of 2 feet is better still, enabling one to identify the small natural undulations which lend themselves to natural green sites and interesting fairway stances.

The topographic character of a "good" property may vary as greatly as do the great courses of the world, from the endless low undulations of St. Andrews to the sweeping hills of Augusta.

The hillier a property, the more acreage is required to come up with a workable course, so that the steepest parts can be avoided in the routing plan. Long slopes of more than 10 percent generally cannot be used within the closely mown area of the course, because the golf ball will continue to roll until it finds a flatter spot. A steep slope might be taken up at the foot of an elevated tee, but it is difficult to account for in other playable areas. There are, of course, many golf holes in the world which exceed this 10-percent rule; only the most ingenious design can overcome the inherent problems, and the resulting holes are bound to be difficult and controversial.

If a course has much more elevation change than 150 feet between high point and low point, it will be very strenuous to walk. Not coincidentally, this is exactly the difference between the clubhouse and the low point, the 11th green, at Augusta National. A greater difference might be workable if the course is stretched out in a line, and all players have the benefit of golf carts. It should be remembered that such a plan eliminates the course from consideration as a venue for top-flight tournament play, when all golfers must walk.

On the other end of the spectrum, nearly flat property combined with ingenious design can also make for a good course as long as it is well drained, naturally or artificially. As Charles Blair Macdonald .pointed out years ago, fairly flat property does offer certain advantages: "The right length of holes can always be adopted; hazards arranged correctly; after that the character of the course depends upon the building of the putting greens." But while a flat course can be made quite interesting, it can never achieve the variety possible in undulating country. Even on a course where money is no object, the scale of golf course construction makes it almost impossible to break free from the lack of variety a simple hill would provide.

It is impossible to describe the character of an ideal property because it can vary so much: the gentle sandhills of Pinehurst No. 2, the abrupt links undulations of Rye, the eskers and kames of Gleneagles, and the dramatic dunes of Royal Birkdale all have their devotees. Simply speaking, the greater the variety of contours and elevations a property contains, the more chance there will be for the architect to differentiate his course from the rest.

Soils

Soil, and the related topic of drainage, is the next item of importance. Sandy loam is the ideal soil for golf: it retains enough moisture to support healthy grass, but also drains well to allow a course to stay open after heavy rains. For the same reason, it reduces construction costs by minimizing delays caused by wet weather. It is no coincidence that fifteen of the top twenty courses in the world are built on sand.

In modern practice, a course can be built on virtually any soil, but construction costs can be very high, and in some cases the soil may prevent turf conditions from achieving a high standard.

Pure sand used to be unworkable for golf, because it was impossible to firmly establish turf without tremendous quantities of topdressing. Today, with large-scale irrigation systems, turf can be established on sand unless its particle size is so uniform that it is mechanically unstable. Most modern greens, in fact, are built on an imported base of pure sand. The natural advantages of good drainage and low per-yard earthmoving expenses are somewhat offset by the quick leaching of fertilizers and chemicals, requiring more frequent applications and greater maintenance expense.

Heavy soils such as clay have more inherent problems. During droughts, unirrigated areas can become dry and cracked, and the ball runs on forever. A drive might even gain distance, by virtue of its error, if the rough is sparse. In wet weather the situation gets out of control. The same pocket-sized undulations which add so much variety to natural courses on sandy soils may trap water and become so soggy that mowing is impossible. Golf-cart traffic will damage the turf. And in the northern latitudes, clays are slow to thaw out in the spring or after a frosty night. Without expensive sub-drainage, all that can be done is to wait for the water to evaporate. Even in good weather, heavy soils support coarser grasses, as opposed to the fine-bladed bents and fescues the golfer prefers.

A particularly costly situation is the presence of shallow rock underlying a course. Excavations on such courses must be carefully calculated to avoid such areas wherever possible; dynamite can also solve the problem, but for a price. Don't forget that the irrigation system must be trenched three feet below the finished grade of the fairways. If part of this will be in rock, the expense will rise astronomically.

With modern technology, it is possible to build a course in an area of solid rock or lava flow. After rough grading, topsoil may either be trucked in and spread at a depth of eight to twenty-four inches, or the rock itself may be crushed to the particle size of fine soil and respread. Such an operation is enormously expensive, adding anywhere from one to ten million dollars to the construction budget, but it is considered part of the cost of doing business in Hawaii and in some other mountainous locales where golf courses could not otherwise exist.

On a parcel of 150 acres or more, it can be expected that a

variety of soils will be found, creating both problems and opportunities for the golf architect and superintendent. Greens should be constructed to provide uniform support conditions for the 18 putting surfaces; if even a few are located in clay, then all will have to be built from the base up. As for fairways, it is usually cost-prohibitive to modify the soil over several acres. The superintendent must often allow for the variety of soils found on the course in his maintenance program. However, a careful analysis of the property with the help of a soil technologist may discover sources of bunker sand, greens mix, clay for lining ponds, or gravel for drainage lines, all of which would help reduce construction costs.

Vegetation

Native vegetation can add immeasurably to the character and beauty of a golf course. A partly wooded property with natural clearings of 100–200 feet in width is ideal for a tree-lined course. Holes can be cleared through the thickest of forests, but trees along the edges of the clearings, previously unexposed to the elements, are subject to great new stresses which may undermine their health. Trees in dense woods also tend to grow upright with little low branching; when exposed during construction, their appearance is much less natural than trees that matured along the edge of an existing clearing.

A property with natural clearings might considerably change the perception of land costs. Clearing through dense woods can cost as much as $3,000 per acre; if another property has natural clearings amenable to golf course routing, the savings might outweigh a higher per-acre land cost.

In analyzing the vegetation of a property, one frequently overlooked feature is the quality of the natural ground cover, whether it be open grassland, ferns or other ground cover, litter under trees, or even desert. If it is of such character that a golf ball can be easily located, and played with some penalty short of damage to the equipment, then by leaving it un-disturbed one can reduce construction costs and the acreage which must be artificially maintained. Many outstanding courses owe much of their character to natural rough areas in marginal areas of play: the new desert courses of Arizona, the wild yucca plants of Prairie Dunes, the heathland courses of southern England, and the pine barrens of Pine Valley. Spe-cial attention must be paid, however, to keeping areas free of destructive traffic during the construction of the course.

Environmental Considerations

Even if all the considerations listed above are ideally suited for golf, it may be impossible to build a course on a given site due to environmental restrictions. Most parts of the civilized world now have some sort of zoning or soil-erosion restrictions re-quiring a permit before work can proceed, opening the door to all sorts of possible obstacles to development. In modern prac-tice, the exploration of these considerations amounts to a legal "discovery" process that can take months or years to complete. A prospective developer should always obtain an option on his selected property, and delay purchase until such process is completed.

The most important environmental consideration is to en-sure that an adequate water supply exists for irrigating the course. A typical course will use between 4,000 and 10,000 gallons of water per acre per day in the heat of the summer, or between 300,000 and 750,000 gallons per day on a course irrigating 75 acres of turf. Natural sources for water such as streams and spring-fed ponds will quickly dry up under such demand; and even if they do not, water-quality biologists advise that no more than 5 percent of the low-water flow is removed, or damage to fish and plants may be significant. Therefore it is usually necessary to locate an underground supply of clean and salt-free well water to supply an irrigation pond.

The use of effluent (treated wastewater) from development sources is becoming increasingly common on golf courses in developing areas of the United States, but the source must be large enough to yield a steady supply when the golf course needs it. Reliance upon municipally provided potable water also has its drawbacks. In times of drought, the golf course may be rationed or cut off from its supply.

The next most common environmental consideration is the presence of wetland areas or floodplains on the property. In the United States such areas are subject to the jurisdiction of the Army Corps of Engineers. Floodplains cannot be graded unless the work is calculated not to increase the downstream flow of water; this means that a course located on a floodplain will be subject to flood damage of varying frequency and intensity. Developers are always anxious to find a valuable use for land which cannot be used for residences or commercial purposes, but such potentially expensive episodes may weigh against the construction of a course on frequently flooded land. Butler National Golf Club in suburban Chicago is a notable example of the pitfalls of floodplain siting.

Wetlands cannot be filled under present statute, although in some states fills may be allowed by permit if mitigated by the creation of new wetlands elsewhere on the site. Wetlands include not only natural bodies of water but marshes, bogs, seasonally flooded lands, or any area where the water table rises to within 6 inches of the surface for more than two weeks per year. In other words, many wetland areas may not be obvious to the untrained eye; since they cannot be filled, they must be accurately located by a specialist to ensure that the golf course plan can be jockeyed around them. This is especially important to modern design, because wetlands represent an unplayable condition and, where they must be carried, the potential grows for holes which are unplayable for the average golfer and which cannot, by law, be fixed satisfactorily.

Just as restrictions on the filling of wetlands have been imposed because of their ecological value in the recharging of groundwater supplies, other ecological and biological consid-erations may restrict the use of a site for a golf course. Property which is considered a valuable wildlife habitat may also have restrictions placed on its use by environmental agencies. A site deemed to have historical or archaeological significance can be ruled off-limits for development as well.

In addition to these wild cards, there is also the possibility that public opposition to growth, most often in a rural area, will result in active opposition to a proposed golf course. Anti-growth factions frequently cloak themselves in the garb of environmentalists, defending the use of the property by any sort of animal or plant as a reason not to develop it for public use, even though the two uses might well coexist. Until the golf industry funds the research to do an exhaustive study of such ecological side effects of golf courses, the presence of public opposition can be a real obstacle to permit approvals, even if their stated objections are vague or unsubstantiated. The burden of proof rests with the developer, though it may be theoretically impossible to "prove" a condition of complete compatibility.

In the modern world, getting a new golf course off the ground can be much more complicated than simply finding ground suited for the purpose.

2

ROUTING
THE COURSE

*"There are 118 golf holes here. All I have to do is
eliminate the 100."*
　　　—PERRY MAXWELL, *on the design of Prairie Dunes.*

The golf architect's primary task is to route the 18 holes to
take the greatest advantage of a property's natural assets. Many
modern courses, relegated to unpromising ground, rely upon
the creative skills of the architect utilizing earthmovers, and
the lay of the land may be of little consequence. On choice
property, architects must discover the correct routing through
the natural terrain, and thereby claim its advantages.

　　The ability to find the "best" routing for a property is a
subjective talent, since no two experts agree as to the composition of an ideal course. But the architect cannot decide upon
his *best* alternative until he has put together several different

schemes. To discover all the potential options is the true skill, and knowledge in two areas is key—the ability to visualize existing features from the topographic maps, and to make mental comparisons with the best holes one has seen or played in the past. The more familiar one is with great courses, the more readily he will be able to visualize similar holes on new property.

Where the architect begins will depend on the priorities of the developer. Often, a resort or housing project is the driving force behind the development of a new course, and land-planning considerations of other land uses will determine where the golf course can be located. Trade-offs are inevitable; however, for the course to be successful, it must be granted a fair share of the prime property. Land-planning firms often relegate the golf course to the back of the lot, depending on it to increase the value of interior parcels, while forgetting that the golf holes can be located on prime ground without disturbing the view from the development. For this reason, it is wise to enlist the services of the golf course architect to work in conjunction with the land planner, before too many boundaries are set.

The golf architect and the land planner have much ground in common, and both start by identifying the most important features of the site. The best potential vistas are located and noted, and ground too steep for construction work is marked off. If there are fine natural clearings of appropriate width for a fairway, then the skeleton of several holes may already be in place, and one begins to look to connect the clearings. Single trees of exceptional beauty are usually worked around once a routing is decided upon.

The golf architect's plan generally revolves around using the topography to make the golf holes interesting. Undulation is the soul of the game; indeed, it is an interesting exercise to reflect on the best holes one has seen or played, and then to realize how many of these great holes are not a product of their bunkering or hazards so much as of the natural contours of the ground. Only then does one begin to appreciate the importance of a good routing plan for the course, because if the routing is good, these undulations do not have to be created.

The first step is to look on the topographic map for areas suitable for green sites and fairway-landing areas. Natural tee sites can also be found, especially where they provide a particularly stunning view. Through tee placement, the architect can bring all golfers to the exact spot he wishes them to see. But tees are least essential, since they are small and can be easily constructed in broken terrain, and since the immediate surroundings of the tee are not "in play."

The ability to read and visualize a topographic map is not a difficult skill, but can only be acquired through practice. To the uninitiated, the contour lines connecting all points at a given elevation appear as a maze; all one can easily discern are the elevations of given points, which can be traced around to the proper number. However, once the high and low points have been sorted out, the experienced eye can distinguish ridges and valleys and saddle points, and begin to visualize the contours of the property. Wooded areas and clearings are also indicated on the topo map.

When working with a relatively flat site, I look first to the places where contour lines are close together, to try and optimize use of the limited natural features. By contrast, on a hilly site, one looks first to where the lines space out, searching for landing areas flat enough to allow the ball to come to rest. A slope of more than 10 percent in a fairway, or 5 percent on a putting green, is generally too steep, and leveling the ground through grading will be impossible if the landing area must be blended into even steeper slopes.

Green sites may be on a natural plateau or at a saddle in the ground, at the crest of a knoll, in a punch bowl or valley, or carved out of a slope (most easily on the flattest part). Natural fairway-landing areas may be in narrow or broad valleys (best entered along the line of the valley itself), at the crest of a ridge (which may be located to control the length of drives, or to

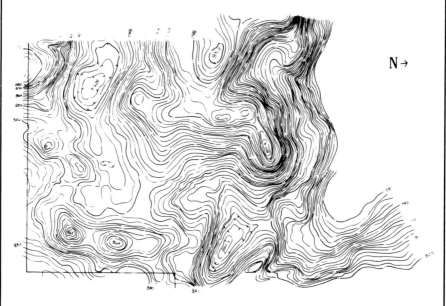

N→

Scale: 1″ = 600 feet

A PORTION OF THE TOPOGRAPHIC MAP
FOR HIGH POINTE G.C.

Primary features to note are the high ridge
running clear along the north side of this portion
of the property, including a promontory (elevation
875.9′) near the center of the ridge, and a shelf at
the far northwest corner; the valley along the
northwest boundary, which is gentle enough to play a
golf hole through; two valleys running east-and-west
through the middle of the area; and the pronounced
ridge on the west side, broad enough for either a
golf hole or housing.

reward a long drive with an extra kick forward), on a suitably gentle slope, or in the midst of gently undulating ground.

Once a green site is discovered, a variety of "natural" golf holes may be considered by tracing back along a visible line of approach to a suitable point for the tee of a short hole or the landing area of a longer hole. In hilly country, cross sections may be made from the topographic map to double-check visibility. The relative size of a natural green site and the surrounding contours may suggest a certain type of hole. For example, a large natural plateau or a punchbowl green site might best be suited to a long par-3 or long two-shot hole, while a site at the top of a steep rise might better be suited to a short pitch, since the slope in front will preclude a running approach. A severe natural hazard or drop to one side of the green site may discourage the design of a long hole, where the player might be likely to find the abyss; or perhaps this would be just the green site for a short par-5, yielding a severe penalty for the strong player who tries, but fails, to get home in two shots.

Not every hole, of course, will feature both a natural green site and landing area; some green sites present only one suitable angle of entry, while others might be approached from many different angles. The ideal is to discover as many holes as possible with at least one natural feature to distinguish them.

Many natural holes may be found on a good piece of property, because the same natural feature might be used in several overlapping schemes. Usually, however, the holes which suggest themselves will form disjointed pieces of a puzzle. The trick is to connect these holes into suitable loops of 9 or 18, either by extending the walks between green and tee, by laying out one or more holes over less than ideal terrain, or by the judicious use of earthmoving equipment to extend the holes or to occupy the space between. In making these transitions, the words of A. W. Tillinghast must be kept close to heart:

> "Often it is necessary to get from one section to another
> over ground which is not suited to easy construction, but

that troublesome hole must be made to stand right up
with the others. If it has nothing about it that might
make it respectable, it has to have quality knocked into
it until it can hold its head up in polite society."

I have found it wise to use natural green sites for the long
holes whenever possible, and to save the short holes to bridge
the gaps between holes, since the gaps may be of odd length.
Also, since a short hole does not require a generous landing
area, it may be artificially constructed much more inexpen-
sively than longer holes. A small green site surrounded by
trouble is best suited to a par-3, since the length of the approach is controlled and the player is guaranteed a reasonable
lie for his approach. A really good natural par-3 hole is a
treasure of design, and should not be passed up; Tillinghast
considered the short holes the keystone of his designs.

On the other hand, it is difficult to find a three-shot hole
that works well in hilly terrain, because dips in the ground may
render the green blind for some approach shots, and Murphy's
Law guarantees that a number of players will have to play their
approaches from just that spot.

Blind shots have been largely eliminated from modern
courses because of safety considerations and liability suits;
most modern designers also agree with Dr. Mackenzie's evaluation that "there may be a certain amount of pleasurable
excitement in running up to the top of a hillock in the hope of
seeing your ball near the flag, but this is the kind of thing one
gets rather tired of as one grows older." Nevertheless, blind
shots have a noble history on the ancient links, and a psychological interest to be explored in chapter 5. More important,
sometimes by relaxing our standards to allow a single blind
shot we are able to provide a dramatic overlook or secure a
much more satisfactory loop of 9 or 18 holes. The blind drive
on Dr. Mackenzie's own fourth hole at Royal Melbourne West
underscores the principle; it not only provides an exciting shot,
but indirectly makes for brilliant 3rd, 5th, and 6th holes as

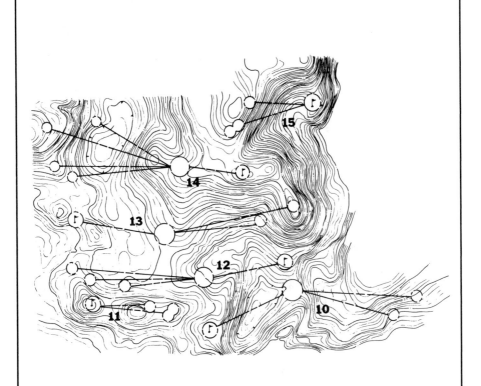

NATURAL GREEN AND TEE SITES—HOLES 10-15
AT HIGH POINTE G.C.

The tenth hole plays into this portion of the property from the north, the only place to access the property without ascending the primary ridge. Green site is at the brink of the hill overlooking the natural bowl. The 12th, 14th, and 15th holes were easily found, with shots across natural valleys to green sites which sit up naturally. This promontory at north center was a perfect tee site, and the saddle between two hills at the south end of the property was an interesting green site for the 13th hole; the sidehill landing arca was not automatically identified, but had to be spaced far enough away from the 12th and 14th. Finally, the 11th hole was made by cutting off the tops of two knobs, and leveling the furthest south to serve as the green site, connecting the 10th and 12th holes.

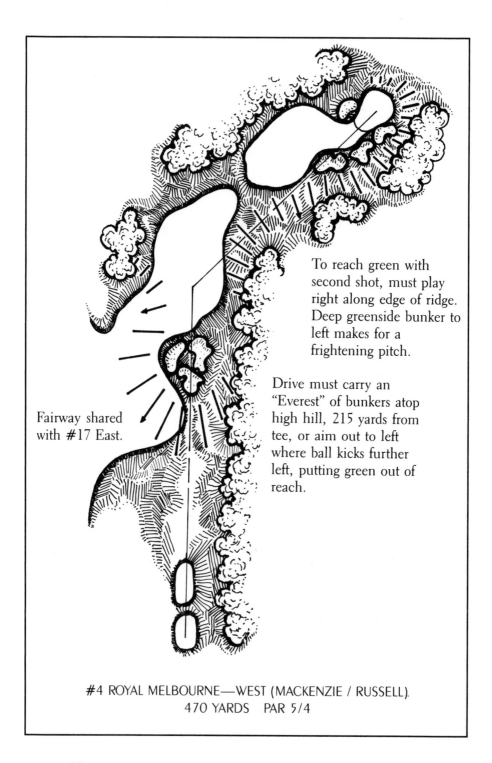

To reach green with second shot, must play right along edge of ridge. Deep greenside bunker to left makes for a frightening pitch.

Drive must carry an "Everest" of bunkers atop high hill, 215 yards from tee, or aim out to left where ball kicks further left, putting green out of reach.

Fairway shared with #17 East.

#4 ROYAL MELBOURNE—WEST (MACKENZIE / RUSSELL).
470 YARDS   PAR 5/4

30

well. Detractors conveniently forget that such great holes as the 8th at Pebble Beach and the Road hole at St. Andrews, generally considered the two best par-4 holes in the world, both incorporate blind tee shots to position the golfer for their unparalleled second shots.

THE CLUBHOUSE

Once the loops of golf holes begin to come together, then and not before should the architect consider the proper location of the clubhouse. The best routing for the course may be overlooked because the clubhouse site was chosen in advance, either because there is an existing building in place or because of the perceived benefits of road access or view. These advantages must be considered, of course, but they are often given too much weight by the developer. In fact, the problems of converting an existing house into a suitable clubhouse are so thorough that the alterations can prove to be a greater expense than the erection of a new structure.

Several considerations apply to the location of the clubhouse, the most important being access to the golf course and room for expansion of facilities. For private clubs it is an advantage, and for daily-fee play it is imperative, to have two or more starting points for the round, usually the 1st and 10th holes. Therefore the clubhouse site must accommodate at least two starting holes, two finishing holes, a practice range, parking, entrance road, and access to electrical supply. If there is the eventual possibility of more golf, additional starting and finishing holes will complicate the plan. These facilities should ideally be spread out in as wide an arc around the clubhouse as possible. If the site is in a corner of the property, or even along one side of the property, the puzzle is far more difficult to solve. Most often the best clubhouse site winds up being near the middle of the property, facilitating two loops of 9 holes spreading out in opposite directions.

If the clubhouse is located on the highest point of the property, it automatically requires a tiring uphill walk on the 9th and 18th holes; since it is difficult to build a good uphill hole, this design cliché is best avoided.

One other consideration is the location of the rising and setting sun: If the clubhouse is located at the western boundary of the property, the starting holes may have to be played into the glare by the early birds of the morning, while the setting sun will hamper visibility on the 18th in the twilight. Even some excellent courses are conspicuous for this failing, including Pebble Beach, where the consolation is that TV cameras looking back down the 18th have perfect lighting. It is best to locate the clubhouse somewhere in the eastern half of the property, or at least in the middle of the site where the architect could be certain to avoid this pitfall.

Sometimes the location of the clubhouse will be obvious to the golf architect and developer. But on other occasions, the confluence of several good holes in the routing process will suggest a site formerly overlooked. It is best to keep an open mind on such matters until the routing is set.

The routing process is a matter of inspiration, and an art unto itself. Sometimes a plan comes together quickly and cannot be ignored. Other times, it seems impossible to obtain the desired twin loops of 9 holes, though great effort should be made before this ideal is abandoned. Typically, several different 18-hole plans are possible. Then it is up to the architect to determine whether one of the alternatives makes for a much better course, or whether the client should be consulted as to nongolfing advantages of the various plans.

In making his choice, the experienced architect will compare not only ideal concepts of golf course routing, but will also use his powers of visualization to compare the potential golf holes in each plan. The fact that there is no one definite solution to the problem makes the architect's experience all the more valuable, and the more time he has to examine the possibilities, the better the course will be.

3

<hr>

ESTHETICS
IN GOLF DESIGN

"No matter how skilfully one may lay out the holes and diversify them, nevertheless one must get the thrill of nature. . . . The puny strivings of the architect do not quench our thirst for the ultimate."
—GEORGE THOMAS, Golf Architecture in America, 1927.

Scratch golfers, who look upon each round of golf as an examination of skill, suggest that the esthetics of the course make no difference to the game, and that any course should be judged purely on its strategic merits. Fortunately, the best golf architects have not paid heed to their opinion. One of the most attractive aspects of the game for the average golfer is the beauty of the surroundings; in fact, when he is playing poorly, it may be the only consolation which brings him back. So why shouldn't we try to build the most beautiful courses we can, as well as the most interesting to play?

The moods of the golf course routing and the character of

the scenery may also have an impact on the golfer's subconscious, where they will affect his play. For example, an
elevated tee excites the golfer, and may tempt him to over-
swing, while a chute of trees off the tee may cause him to
constrain his backswing. The British golfer who has grown up
on wide-open links courses often gets a sense of claustrophobia
on a wooded course, and drives into the trees all day. The
American golfer who has grown up on a wooded course often
feels lost on the links, without trees to visually define the limits
of the hole and give him a comfortable closed space in which
to drive the ball.

Beauty, of course, is in the eye of the beholder. For the
golfer, the acid test is that the visual elements jibe with the
strategy of the golf hole. A stream flowing across a fairway is
beautiful, but not if it crosses right where your drive would
land. One of Dr. Mackenzie's favorite stories was of the caddie
who, when asked the members' opinion of a particular water
hazard, noted: "Weel, we've got an old Scotch major here.
When he gets it over he says, 'Weel over the bonnie wee burn,
ma laddie'; but when he gets in he says 'Pick ma ball oot o' that
damned sewer.'"

Another aspect of beauty is continuity of character, and this
can separate the truly great courses from the merely admirable
ones. Most of the great courses of the world have a visual
character all their own. The Old Course at St. Andrews draws
its character from the town, where it begins and ends, whose
major buildings serve as landmarks in choosing a line of play
on the incoming holes, as well as from its unique double
fairways and double greens, which bring adjacent holes into
play. At Pine Valley, by contrast, each hole is isolated by trees,
but the course impresses at first glance because of its grand
scale: bold hazards, great undulations, with expansive fairways
and greens to complete the picture, and make it practical to
play. Augusta National, Royal Melbourne, the National Golf
Links of America, Desert Highlands, Royal St. George's, and
Royal County Down are perhaps the only other courses in the
world to be built at such a scale and to carry it through suc-

cessfully. Conversely, such courses as Merion, Kingston Heath, and Inverness are confined to small properties, and the intricacy of the greens contouring and bunkering is kept in scale with the rest of the picture.

The greatest courses do not simply fall back on the natural beauty of the property, but are designed to *enhance* the beauty of the property by directing the golfer around the property to see it in all its aspects, and by adding features that blend into the landscape while helping to focus the golfer's view. In each aspect of golf course design, from routing the course to hazard placement to the construction of bunkers and greens, there is opportunity for the sympathetic golf architect to add to the beauty of the landscape.

In routing the course, the first goal should be to explore the property and to direct the golfer to its most dramatic spots. Pebble Beach and Casa de Campo have their dramatic stretches of oceanside holes, while Ballybunion wanders in and out of the dunes, keeping the golfer wondering when his next encounter with the ocean will come. One of my favorite examples of routing is at Herbert Fowler and Tom Simpson's Cruden Bay in Scotland. The course begins with three holes below the town's main street, turns to the sea alongside Cruden Water at the wonderful par-3 4th, and then plows through huge dunes for three long holes. Then the routing crosses over itself into the huge amphitheater of the 8th hole; you walk up out of the links ground to play across the domed field of the long 9th; drop dramatically back to the links and play out to the far end at the 12th green; run the narrow gauntlet between the dunes and the high hill from the 14th through 16th holes, completing the southern loop of the figure-eight routing; and finally head inland to finish below the clubhouse. The genius of all this is that the golf course is routed exactly the way you might be inclined to wander the property if there were no golf course there. Royal Dornoch and Fishers Island are two other wonderful examples of this aspect of routing.

Perhaps the best study of golf course esthetics is Dr. Mackenzie's Cypress Point. The property is a dramatic mixture of oceanside, open, and wooded terrain, yet it had the potential to be a fragmented course if the routing had simply followed several holes in one terrain with several in another. Instead, Mackenzie's routing wanders across open ground, back into the cypress trees, out onto the high prospect of the 8th and 9th holes, back into and out of the trees, back across the open ground with the ocean in view, and finally to its dramatic cliff-top climax, mixing up the scenery to make it flow together.

Mackenzie also had a unique talent for finding a variety of backdrops for his green sites, and possibly no course in the world offers a more dramatic example than the back 9 at Cypress Point. A quick summary would go as follows:

10th. Uphill approach, short grass behind green rising gently to pine trees.

11th. Downhill approach, green at foot of a towering sand dune behind.

12th. Sidehill green site dropping to the left, with view straight through to the ocean in the distance behind the green.

13th. Plateau green set into the side of a dune, dropping off to the right.

14th. High green set against the sky, framed left and right by cypress trees in the foreground, but undefended by bunkers.

15th. Surrounded by bunkers of all shapes and sizes, backed up by a dense, dark stand of cypresses.

16th. Green on the tip of the peninsula, looking straight out to the ocean.

17th. Green again jutting out from the shore, but looking down along the coastline.

18th. Elevated green with sky behind, looking up under the trunks of cypresses on either side.

Mackenzie also succeeded in blending bunkers and greens into the landscape. His bunkers were dramatic flashes of sand with fringed edges in harmony with both the jagged profiles of the cypress trees on the front 9 and the rocky coastline of the final holes; the lines of the bunkers on the open holes are more subdued. For an architect well-known for dramatically contouring his greens, the putting surfaces of Cypress Point are deliberately subdued. With all the dramatic views, I believe Mackenzie must have decided not to compete with the scenery in his design.

Where the scenery is less dramatic, the architect may add visual interest in the detailing of greens and bunkers, but this is where most modern architects fall short. Modern construction methods have granted them the power to introduce all sorts of landscape features, from trees to mounds to ponds to waterfalls, but too often today's architects rely on these extraneous features in lieu of elements integral to the play—the bunkers and contours of the green. Both Tillinghast and Tom Simpson had observations on this phenomenon:

> "A round of golf should present 18 inspirations—not necessarily thrills, because spectacular holes may be sadly overdone. Every hole may be constructed to provide charm without being obtrusive about it. When I speak of a hole being inspiring, it is not intended to imply that the visitor is to be subject to attacks of hysteria on every teeing ground. It must be remembered that the great majority of golfers are aiming to reduce their previous best performance by five strokes if possible, and if any one of them arrives at the home teeing ground with this possibility in reach, he is not caring too much whether he is driving off from a nearby ancient oak of majestic size, or from a dead sassafras. If his round ends happily, this is one beautiful course. Such is human nature."
>
> —A. W. TILLINGHAST

> "The educated taste admires simplicity of design and sound workmanship for their own sake rather than overdecoration and the crowding of artificial hazards."
>
> —WETHERED and SIMPSON,
> *The Architectural Side of Golf.*

Unfortunately, the few modern architects who profess to imitate the classics have generally erred on the side of conservatism, if not dullness. It is important to remember that the courses accepted today as classics were once considered radical. Their artificial features have softened and blended into the landscape over sixty years of existence, to the point where few observers realize how much artificial work was done in their construction. Pine Valley, to cite an extreme example, was six years in the making; even the islands in the sandy hazards such as Hell's Half Acre were artificially constructed, though most golfers mistake them for being natural hazards. They also have to be carefully maintained to prevent erosion or thickening of the undergrowth, belying their reputation as "unmaintained hazards."

It is critical to recognize that while it is important not to overdo artificial construction, where construction is necessary, enough dirt must be moved to disguise the work. It is the early Victorian golf architecture of turn-of-the-century Britain and America, replete with geometric and unnatural bunkering, which represents the minimum-construction approach. In contrast, on the classic courses we revere, the green complexes and bunkers were often the product of weeks' work with teams of mules or horses, and manual labor. The architects were successful in disguising their artificial work by making their cuts and fills in flowing contours, now largely indistinguishable to the untrained eye. Such work is best accomplished in the field rather than in plans, since it is most successful when the contractor imitates the flow of surrounding natural contours, as a sculptor would.[1]

It must be admitted that the standards of modern construction have made it more difficult for the architect to work with the land. To cite just a few examples:

---

[1]It is the contours of the immediate surroundings which should be emulated in artificial construction work; some architects have gone to the point of mimicking the rise and fall of distant mountains in their mounding behind greens, but Nature seldom carries harmony to this extent.

1. Greens built to top-of-the-line specifications must be created in three perfect layers, giving the architect little latitude to change the final surface to suit the eye, and making it much more difficult to create the subtle folds at the edges of greens which are found on older courses.

2. The need to create an irrigation reservoir often saddles the course with one or two water holes, potentially incongruous in the desert or on a links-style course.

3. The common practice of shaping the fairways with pans and bulldozers removes all the subtle pockets and folds in the ground, a source for interesting lies and stances. The recently popular style of elevated fairways with sharp edges to create shadows is particularly offensive, for it creates not only an unnatural look but playability problems and maintenance nightmares.

4. The plague of motorized golf carts has required architects to find ways to hide cart paths in the landscape, requiring the addition of much artificial mounding and adding a major expense to the budget.

5. The high-tech methods of collecting and recirculating drainage water from the golf course, and modern environmental restrictions limiting the impact of the course on natural features such as wetlands, has led architects to resort to increasingly artificial-looking design solutions; if golf courses were less artificially maintained, such construction would be largely unnecessary.

Despite these difficulties, much of the blame for the predictability of modern courses rests with architects and developers without the patience to wait for growth or the imagination to try new things. Aggressive landscaping has produced dramatic results, from C. B. Macdonald's now-defunct Lido

Golf Club, the first and best artificial "links," to the new pine forest and rushing streams of Shadow Creek. We forget today just how many of our beautiful U. S. Open courses, from Oak Hill to Olympic, were originally barren farms landscaped by far-sighted committees.

VARIETY, THE SPICE OF GOLF COURSES

It is impossible to quantify what makes a great golf course. It is easy enough to come up with a list of principles of sound design: The course should be playable for all levels of golfers, yet difficult enough to interest the better players; the course should work with the given topography to the utmost, and all artificial features should blend into the landscape unobtrusively; the holes should always reward good play; and the course should be easily maintainable.

Yet the great courses stand apart because of their differences from the rest, not because they adhere to some definition of "greatness" more than the others.

The problem with most courses is that we pay too much attention to false idols of "good" design, such as length, difficulty, balance, and setting, and lose sight of the underlying principle that the best golf course is the one with the greatest variety in all facets of its design.

The golf course with the widest variety of holes has everything. It will be a fair course, because it is not designed around one particular shot pattern, and lets all players demonstrate their golfing skills. It should attain a modicum of balance, simply by avoiding a repetitive string of holes following a similar pattern. The individuality of the holes will create a "flow" to the sequence of play, similar to the musical score of a film, creating a mood for the course. And a truly well-varied routing plan will ensure that the wind exerts its influence from a variety of angles, that the course explores the interesting corners of the property, and that the visual aspect of the course changes from hole to hole.

Certainly the question of whether the course is intended for municipal, private, resort, or tournament play has some bearing on the design and on the layout of facilities, but too much of a distinction has been drawn by golf architects over the years in their planning. Unfortunately, many architects have aimed low in their designs of public courses, passing over potentially dramatic holes on the grounds they would be too difficult for the beginner or too expensive to maintain, instead of working to make them playable for less expert golfers. Nothing is needed more in golf today than affordable courses on which new players might learn the game; but the assumption that such courses must be void of design interest is wrong. The difference between a good course and a mediocre one can't be blamed on the construction budget but rather the lack of attention to detail on the part of the architect. If little attempt is made to build an interesting course for beginners, how will they ever learn to appreciate the game?

Meanwhile, on tournament courses, architects have become so preoccupied with making the course difficult that some have excluded the short par-4 holes calling for finesse, and making the game bearable for weaker players.

The less said about the ideal length or par of a course, the better. Some people become preoccupied with trying to achieve an arbitrary standard of par 72, or a back-tee length of 7,000 yards, and sacrifice the best potential golf holes because they do not fit into such a scheme. In choosing a routing, the architect should look on each natural hole he discovers as a precious resource and try to include as many of these as possible in the final layout, whatever the sum total of par or yardage.

The important thing is to design a variety of holes calling for strength, accuracy, and finesse. This can be achieved on a course much shorter than 7,000 yards. A fine example is Harry S. Colt's Swinley Forest, in England. Strict par is 68 (although the club lists only the "bogey" score on the card, refusing to follow the convention of par), with five short holes and only one three-shotter, and the total length is just 6,001 yards. Yet the course seems quite difficult, because of several stout two-shotters. Another designer might have been tempted to stretch some of these into short par-5 holes to make par a more standard figure, but then the slightly longer course would likely have been pronounced "too easy" in relation to par.

In fact, a par-68 or par-70 course makes it easier for the average player to break 80 (or 90 or 100), but harder for the good player to break par, since it cuts out some of the par-5 holes which provide the easiest birdie opportunities. Simultaneously, the short course reduces the acreage of required land and of fairway to be maintained, keeping the budget in line. On the other hand, some of our greatest courses—including The National, Garden City, and Royal Portrush—are par-73. So who's to say that "even fours" is the only solution?

A balanced course should be arranged to allow all players the chance to demonstrate particular golfing skills, and to force them to confront their weaknesses; the course should have enough variety that no player is unduly favored. The architect must be extremely careful not to inject the strengths of his own game into the equation, or the course will favor players with similar strengths. Many modern designers have made this mistake by visualizing approach shots to greens strictly as aerial shots from a perfect lie in the fairway, when in fact average golfers may play their approach from many distances or angles. It is acceptable to confront the weak player with an occasional carrying approach, so he is forced to work on his game; but by giving scope for the running approach as well as the aerial, we can keep the average golfer in the game.

Practically speaking, there ought to be approximately the same number of hazards to the right as to the left, and a balance of doglegs on each side as well as some straightaway holes. Nevertheless, the desire for balance should not outweigh the lay of the land. It would be folly to build a poor dogleg to the right to improve the balance of the course if there exists a good natural green site to the left. In fact, a careful analysis of the great courses reveals many an imbalance: The Old Course at St. Andrews has the majority of its driving hazards on the right, while Ballybunion Old has eight doglegs to the left, and only two to the right.

Some old designers theorized that the majority of hazards should be on the right of the course to punish the slicer (one famous advocate was Herbert Fowler, the designer of Walton Heath), while more forgiving modern designers tend to concentrate their hazards on the left because the weaker player already has enough trouble. Neither theory must be overused, or the architect will be favoring one player over another.

The final obstacle to variety is the architect's set of design prejudices. The more courses an architect has built, the more refined his ideas of correct design become, to the point that he starts to build refinements of his earlier courses instead of working with each given property from a fresh perspective. This may help to explain why so many of our truly great courses—Pine Valley, Merion, Oakmont, Pebble Beach, The National, and Woodhall Spa—are the work of amateur or first-time architects, who brought fresh ideas to their work. These examples serve to make the work of the few great architects with long careers (Colt, Mackenzie, Ross, Tillinghast) that much more impressive.

Within the framework of balance, it is the goal of the golf architect to build holes calling for a variety of shots and arranged so that there is sufficient change of character from one hole to the next.

A degree of variety is automatically obtained since holes are divided into par-3's, par-4's, and par-5's, and further differentiated by length within those categories. But this is overly simplistic. When Dr. Mackenzie wrote in 1920 that "every hole should have a different character," he did not mean that one should be marked by a waterfall, one by a horseshoe-shaped green, and so on; nor did he mean that the lengths of the two-shot holes should be graduated in ten-yard increments, to "make the player hit every club in the bag." In fact, this is a fruitless pursuit, since average golfers do not drive the ball a consistent distance, while the best players make the same swing with a five-iron as a seven. Mackenzie simply meant that there should be a variety of holes, some severe, some benign.

The variety between the holes can be enhanced by the sequence in which they are played. As in a musical composition, it is important not to follow any pattern repetitively. For example, if the golf course is to be built in a windy climate, then the architect must take extra care to avoid long stretches of holes played in one direction, or a procession of parallel holes running back and forth, like targets in a carnival shooting gallery; either plan becomes monotonous in a strong wind. One technique popular in the 1920's was to arrange the holes in triangular patterns: One hole would play to the north, a second to the southeast, and the third back westerly to the first tee, where a new loop would begin.

Another common mistake is to simply alternate the pars of the holes, as in the front 9 at Augusta National—4, 5, 4, 3, 4, 3, 4, 5, 4. Such a superficial analysis does not tell us anything about the various characters of the holes. For example, at Augusta the flow of holes is from a hard no. 1, to an easy 2nd and 3rd, to a difficult 4th and 5th, and then to another easy stretch, instead of the simple beat suggested by the sequence of pars. More importantly, by sticking to a rigid formula the architect would have to ignore other routings with perhaps better natural holes. Mackenzie's Cypress Point, with consecutive par-5 holes on the front 9 and the famous short par-3 15th and long par-3 16th back-to-back, is the classic example that such formulas need not carry the day.

Housing-development courses in hilly terrain and modern "stadium" courses also suffer from an imposed lack of variety, when the developer thinks more about the frame than the

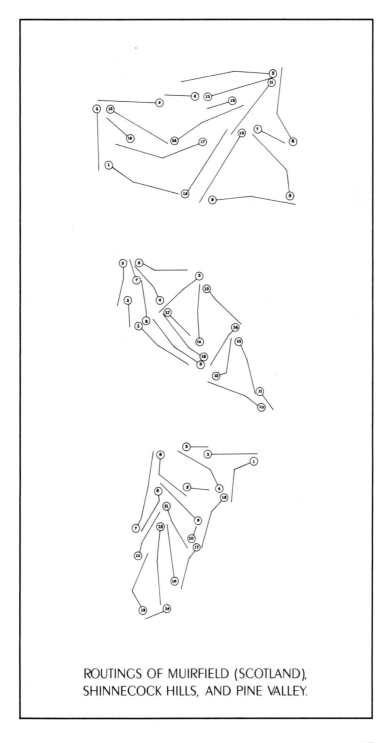

ROUTINGS OF MUIRFIELD (SCOTLAND),
SHINNECOCK HILLS, AND PINE VALLEY.

picture. Any course confined exclusively to valleys pales in comparison to a routing which wanders over hill and dale. While good views for spectators are important on a tournament course, it is ridiculous for such considerations to outweigh the design of an interesting test of golf.

The call for variety can be extended to almost any aspect of golf course design. The architect should provide not only for approaches of different lengths, but also for approaches which call for different *shots* (fade, draw, pitch, and run-up) from a variety of stances. The scenery and strategy of the holes can also be used by the master architect to create different moods on the course and different thoughts in the player's mind, while the golfer tries to concentrate on playing his own game instead of being lured into trying foolish shots because of the course or his opponent's position. We will explore the variety of shotmaking, of strategy, and of psychology in the next few chapters, as all have their place in proper design.

4

FAIR PLAY

"[The chief virtues of the links] may briefly be summarized as being: first, that they should be difficult; secondly, that they should be pleasing to the eye; thirdly, that they should be strictly economical in design; and lastly, that to be truly admirable they will probably incur in the general opinion the accusation of being unfair."
—H. N. WETHERED, The Perfect Golfer, 1931.

The most common criticism levelled at a golf course is that some difficult hole is "unfair." But how do we define the term? Fairness, too, is in the eye of the beholder.

Scratch golfers believe they have special province to judge the fairness of golf holes, because the accepted measure of difficulty—the par value of each hole—is based on the scratch player's expected score. Architect Robert Trent Jones reinforced this belief when he pronounced that "every hole should be a hard par but an easy bogey," obviously with the scratch player in mind. For the 36-handicapper, no hole is an easy bogey.

By the standard of par value, many of the celebrated holes in the game would have to be judged as unsatisfactory. Who could defend the Road hole at St. Andrews as a "fair" par-4, with a blind drive across out-of-bounds and just a few yards of green between the dreaded Road bunker and the pavement on its rear flank? If the hole were just twenty yards longer and called a par-5, it would undoubtedly be much less controversial, even though it was more difficult by virtue of its added length. By the same token, a short par-4 would have to be defended as severely as the 8th at Pine Valley to equal the difficulty of a standard 420-yard par-4, while the classic short par-5 such as the 13th at Augusta National would fail the test for playing too easily, relative to par.

All of these are recognized as great holes, not because they are difficult or easy to par but because they make for interesting and competitive play from tee to green. In match play, their par makes no difference—the golfer's fate is relative only to his opponent's score for the hole. It is less universally understood, however, that the same rule applies for medal play, because every competitor plays the hole an equal number of times.

Competitive play is a small part of golf, but in recreational play, par has even less meaning. Even the two-handicapper expects to make a couple of bogeys along the way; only the scratch golfers judge themselves against par, and even then, they expect the birdies and bogeys to balance out. Golfers judge themselves not against par but against their own expectations, or by the measure of fun derived from the game.

Golf is no more fair than life in general. One of the qualities of golf that is supposed to build personal character is the need to put one's failures or poor luck behind and concentrate on the next shot. So, it is only natural that on the golf course, as in life, some holes are more difficult than others. Scratch players may declare a hole unfair when they are faced with shots beyond their ability, but average golfers frequently face the same dilemma.

It is also part of golf as the Scots invented it that the "rub of the green" plays a part in the game, and that the player who has the mental resiliency to overcome a bad bounce or bad lie is ultimately rewarded. American golf has almost eliminated this element by overwatering courses so that an approach shot stops immediately upon landing, but the philosophy of the British game is still much the same as it was stated years ago:

> "The perfect shot is invariably rewarded; it is only right
> that the shot which is slightly imperfect should be
> weighed in the scales of providence."
> —H. N. WETHERED, *The Perfect Golfer*, 1931.

Though the golfer never admits it, there are lucky bounces as well as unlucky ones, and these also play an important role in the game. The golfer must learn to capitalize on his own good fortune, while not letting the good luck of his opponent get under his skin. Meanwhile, both good bounces and bad add interest and emotion to the game.

The golf architect's role cannot and should not be as the ultimate arbiter of fairness. He should seek only to get the most out of the ground in his holes, while letting the play take care of itself by arranging the course so that talent at any one aspect of the game—driving, iron play, short game, and putting—should not usurp the need to be skilled in other aspects. Each hole must be carefully designed to balance risk and reward, to balance such factors as the width of the fairway versus the severity of the rough, and the size of the green with the circumstances of the approach shot. As Bobby Jones put it in *Golf Is My Game*, "each player must be given something to do, and that something must be within the realm of reasonable accomplishment." This is the simplest definition of "shot values."

Shot values would be simple to arrange if all golfers were equally talented. In practice they are a much more complex matter, because players differ considerably in their abilities. As an example, let us examine a straightaway 360-yard par-4 hole. Without wind or topography as a factor, the modern Tour professional can be expected to hit his drive 260–275 yards, leaving him a pitch of under 100 yards to the green. For such a golfer, a 3,000-square-foot green would be none too small. But the average player, whose solid drive will travel 210 yards, will often drive only 185, leaving him with a medium to long iron shot to the green. If the green is big enough for this golfer, the professional will find the hole dull; if it is only big enough for the professional, the average golfer will find the hole impossible.

It is foolish to lay out a hole or design a green based on how any one player will face it. The goal is to design the hole so that it will not only remain playable, but also retain its interest, no matter where the golfer might find himself on the way to the green. Or, in Dr. Mackenzie's words, each hole should be fun for everybody, "irrespective of whether they are piling up a big score." It is interesting to note that most golfers cannot form an objective opinion about a course if they have played it badly; where they hit a poor tee shot they probably never saw any of the key features of the hole.

So there is no ideal green size for an approach of 160 yards, because by no means will everyone face an approach of that length. A 4,000-square-foot green could be appropriate, if there is space around it where the average golfer might miss the green without being harshly penalized. A 10,000-square-foot green could be equally appropriate, if divided by contours so that it provides sufficient small-scale interest for recovery shots by those who missed the green. The choice depends as much on personal style and physical requirements as any objective standard of fairness.

The only hole rightly judged as unfair is one the poorer golfer may never finish, because it calls for a forced carry beyond his means over an unplayable hazard, such as water. As the late Bernard Darwin wrote of the 8th at Pine Valley, "it is all well and good to punish a bad shot, but the right of eternal punishment should be reserved for a higher tribunal than a green committee."

While no single hole can be judged unfair as long as there is room to avoid its hazards, over the course of 18 holes a different standard of fairness must be used. The course that repeatedly punishes one type of shot, hole after hole, can legitimately be criticized as unfair, at least by the golfer who relies on that particular shot.

The most common example of unfairness is the course designed under the assumption that there is some magic distance at which fairway bunkers should be placed, based on the average driving length of the Tour professional or the average golfer of the day. No matter the caliber of player involved, individuals at the same overall level of skill hit the ball different distances off the tee. It is absurd to place fairway bunkers to penalize one player more than the other. The only fair solution to the positioning of fairway bunkers is to avoid any repetition of distances.

To illustrate the point, imagine a best-ball match in which the reader and Jack Nicklaus are pitted against Nancy Lopez and Lee Trevino. In theory, this ought to be a fairly even match; if it was played on a course which required 200-yard carries from every tee, the reader would be at a disadvantage, and if played on a course requiring 240-yard carries, it would be unfair because only Nicklaus could drive that far. Does not the same consideration apply to a course where all the fairway bunkers are 225 yards from the tee? And if our fictitious match were played on a Robert Trent Jones–designed course, with fairway bunkers pinching the landing areas 240–270 yards from every tee, would not the reader cry "foul" because the course does not allow his partner to use the driver?

Other types of unfair design include courses that repeatedly demand a high, soft shot onto the green—a shot which the average player simply does not possess—and courses where the designer visualizes his own draw or fade as the preferred approach to the greens, and lays out his hazards to favor one over the other.

If the architect is sure to champion variety in his design, then criticisms of the course as unfair will be recognized as the venting of frustration. Every course worth its salt prompts a certain amount of sour grapes.

5

THE PSYCHOLOGY
OF DESIGN

" . . . *But reduce the dimensions of the target and give it
a slightly unusual or unexpected shape, and the chances
are that the ball will not be laid within twice the distance
from the pin that it would otherwise have found, although
the shot, so far as the position of the pin is concerned, is
precisely the same in either case. The shot follows the eye
and the line of thought. . . . An impending sense of
misfortune will almost certainly be reflected in the action
of the club.*"

—WETHERED and SIMPSON,
The Architectural Side of Golf, 1929.

"When you get those dudes thinking, they're in trouble."
—PETE DYE, 1985.

Every golfer knows that the game requires more than physical talent. Anyone can learn to hit the ball with reasonable
proficiency; the key to success is to do it with consistency.
Since the golf swing happens so fast, our control of it is largely
subconscious. It should come as no surprise that golf architecture also has a distinct psychological element.

The most common phobia among golfers is a fear of water hazards, even if the location should not cause them to think twice. A carry of 100 yards is readily accomplished by most golfers, but how much more often do we top our drive when there is a pond just in front of the tee? Our failure isn't really that we prematurely looked up, it is the fear of making fools of ourselves and self-doubt that makes our swing go haywire.

The clever golf architect understands the psychology of the game, and exploits it in his design in a variety of ways. The architect who wished only to give the average golfer his best mathematical chance against the professional would build no hazards at all, since they weigh more heavily on the psyche of the weaker player. That would take all the fun out of the game, as Dr. Mackenzie recognized in *Golf Architecture*:

> "One of the objects in placing hazards is to give the play-ers as much pleasurable excitement as possible. . . .
>
> "It is an important thing in golf to make holes look much more difficult than they really are. People get more pleasure in doing a hole which looks almost impossible, and yet is not so difficult as it appears.
>
> "In this connection it may be pointed out that rough grass is of little interest as a hazard. It is frequently much more difficult than a fearsome-looking bunker or belt of whins or rushes, but it causes considerable annoyance in lost balls, and no one ever gets the same thrills in driving over a stretch of rough as over a fearsome-looking bunker, which in reality may not be so severe."

It was not lost on Mackenzie that by building such hazards, the average golfer's confidence would grow as he progressed through the round, even more so if he should occasionally land in a bunker and find that it was not as difficult as he had imagined. Instead of using psychology to defeat the good play-er, Mackenzie's courses inspire the average golfer.

Mackenzie was probably the first golf architect with the perspective of providing fun for the average golfer, as opposed to meting out strict justice to shots played. He knew there must not be impossible carries to frustrate the golfer, but that there had to be enough formidable hazards to excite the golfer. He knew there had to be some potential birdie holes—par-3 holes and short par-4's—to encourage the weaker player, and that the beauty of the golf course could inspire and console the golfer off his game.

To extend the principle, Mackenzie's courses are always sure to include at least a couple of short par-4 holes—relatively easy from the standpoint of par value. Their psychological effect on two classes of golfers, however, is far different. The short par-4 gives the average player a realistic chance at a par or a birdie, and may boost his confidence for the more difficult holes ahead. But the Tour professional expects to make birdies on easy holes, and puts pressure on himself in the process. If he misses his birdie on a short par-4, he may lose his concentration; if a series of tougher holes follows, his frustration may lead to bogeys.

The absence of hazards on a hole can also have unexpected effects in competition, because of the different ways in which different golfers perceive a hazard. The poorer player sees the hazard, imagines all the trouble lying in wait, and has difficulty freeing his mind to make a normal swing. The accomplished player focuses in on his target, and as long as it is reasonably sized for the length of the shot to be played, surrounding it with bunkers only serves to help him concentrate on his target more clearly. When there is no guardian hazard, the situation is reversed: The poorer player is relieved and may hit his shot right up to the hole, but the accomplished player may have more difficulty visualizing the shot he wants to play because there are no landmarks to assist him.

The accomplished player's consistency from 100 yards in suggests a radically different approach to designing the short par-4. With a wedge in hand, most hazards are window dressing for the Tour player. His target is a circle ten or fifteen feet around the hole, and no hazard could be closer than that. So why surround the green with hazards? To give the poorer golfer a breather by leaving him a fairly easy, open approach, and hope that the professional gets frustrated if he misses his birdie, since he would probably make his par 95 times out of 100, no matter what hazards are put around the target.

The 7th hole at High Pointe, my first solo design, nicely illustrates this point. The drive can be difficult for the better player who wants to avoid a semi-blind approach by hitting past the bowl in the fairway; but the green is completely open to the running approach, giving the weak player a chance to recover from even the poorest drive. The deep pot bunker hidden behind the green is a bonus: The weaker player often forgets it is even there, but the better player fears the hazard he cannot see, and often fails to get his approach back to the hole.

The same principle applies not only to long approaches, but to short chips and pitches around the greens. When the grass grows high around the greens the player has no choice but to pitch his ball back onto the putting surface, and the better pitcher fares better. Mow the apron down to fairway height, as at St. Andrews, Augusta, or Royal Dornoch, and even modest contours now add tremendous interest to the play. The master of the short game may putt up a steep bank onto the green, or chip a ball into the bank and let it expire after its first bounce carries it up onto the green, instead of pitching onto the green with the fear that a short shot will roll back to him. But the player who is not naturally talented in these shots may talk himself into playing a low-percentage shot to try to get close to the hole, risking a higher score than if he had simply played a straightforward pitch safely past the hole.

One of the most frustrating things about the Old Course at St. Andrews is that the player who knows the course best may think too much about how he might best get close to the hole, and miss the green entirely. The great courses entice the golfer to outwit himself.

Another excellent use of psychology is the green site which appears heavily defended on one side and open on the other, such as the first green at Pinehurst No. 2. With a deep bunker

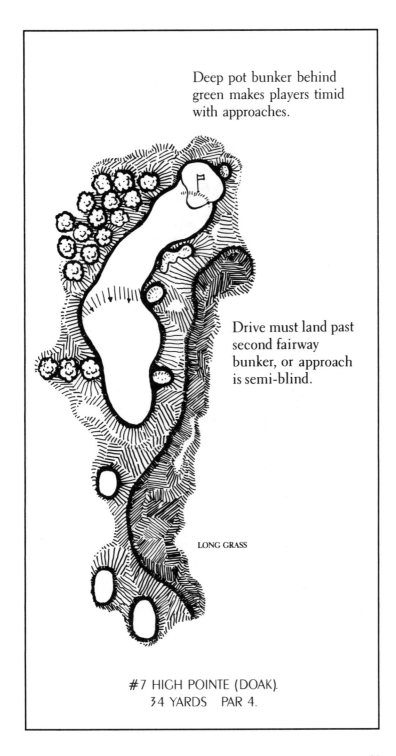

Deep pot bunker behind green makes players timid with approaches.

Drive must land past second fairway bunker, or approach is semi-blind.

LONG GRASS

#7 HIGH POINTE (DOAK).
34 YARDS   PAR 4.

Deep bunker on left, but tilt of green makes recovery easier. Offset fairway to right lures a timid approach, but leaves player a difficult chip.

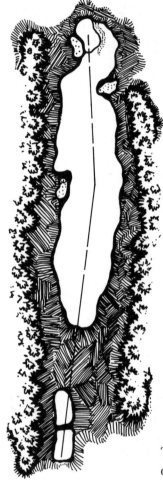

Tees aligned with treeline on left.

#1 PINEHURST—NO. 2 COURSE (ROSS).
414 YARDS   PAR 4

to the left of the green and short grass to the right, good players
with less than stout hearts may be tempted to hedge to the
right and draw the ball in to the target, secure in the knowledge that a straight shot will escape unscathed. They will make
fewer birdies in the process. Meanwhile, weaker players could
also play to the "bail-out" area when faced with a long approach, leaving them the chance to get up and down for a
half. If the architect is extremely clever, as Donald Ross certainly was, he will contour the green so that the chip from the
right of the green is more difficult than it appears from the
fairway. Meanwhile, the bunker shot the player was trying to
avoid might have been relatively simple.

I suspect that building green sites surrounded by hazards on
our modern tournament courses has inadvertently helped golfers with less intestinal fortitude by giving them no choice but
to aim at the flagstick. Given the chance to hedge their shots to
a safe area, these golfers might shoot higher scores by being
less daring, and more instinctively aggressive golfers would fare
better.

Just as the weaker player welcomes the occasional easy hole,
the best players welcome an especially difficult hole or two
within the 18, to test them to the limit and distinguish them
from the merely good player. Such holes also have an attrac-
tion for the weaker golfer who plays for enjoyment: They offer
him the opportunity to play a single shot that will redeem an
otherwise forgettable round. A par on such a hole as the 16th
at Cypress Point can be the highlight of a lifetime of golf.

The design of difficult holes provides the architect an opportunity to break away from the strictures of designing "fair"
holes around par values, and gives the average player a competitive chance. On a long two-shot hole with a large green,
the average player who cannot get home in two has a fairly
boring third shot to play, with little chance of getting his four;
the good player who misses the green with his second has a
good chance of getting up and down for his par. Make the
green less receptive, such as on the Road hole at St. Andrews,

and the good player must struggle to save par and keep an edge over the weaker player who gets home in three. At the same time, only a truly great approach shot working right to left will get close to the hole for a birdie try, presenting the opportunity for the best players in the world to display their full range of talents.

The order in which the architect arranges his holes may also be devised for psychological impact. One example is the "killer hole" golfers especially fear, such as the island 17th of the TPC at Sawgrass. In tournament play, the knowledge that this hole must be faced, and that there is no way to play the hole safely, may cause a leader to take risks early in the round to pad his lead. Even if he is successful, the more he worries about the hole during his round, the more effect the pressure will have on him when he confronts the hole.

We have seen how a difficult hole can be tougher when followed by an easy hole. The so-called tournament finish, where the holes get progressively more difficult, is an extension of the same theory. The long par-4 finishing hole flanked by water has become almost a cliché of modern design, forcing the player to resist the temptation to choke right up to the finish.

My preference is for a course that builds to an extremely difficult 17th hole, but offers something of a respite at the 18th. This is a pattern often found on British links, perhaps because when golfers played almost exclusively in matches, architects were afraid that a heroic 18th hole might never be used. I prefer a course that gives the tournament golfer a chance to finish with a heroic winning birdie, instead of either hanging on with a four or losing the tournament to a man in the clubhouse with a final bogey. The finishing hole at Royal Lytham & St. Annes, with an extremely tough tee shot between bunkers, but short enough to give hope for a birdie if the drive is good, is to my mind the ideal tournament finish, especially when coupled with the difficult, long 17th hole.

Another psychological trap of golf architecture is the blind

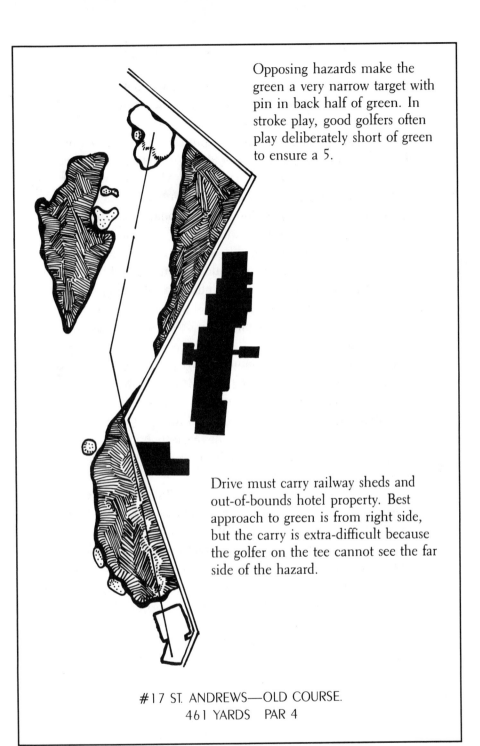

Opposing hazards make the green a very narrow target with pin in back half of green. In stroke play, good golfers often play deliberately short of green to ensure a 5.

Drive must carry railway sheds and out-of-bounds hotel property. Best approach to green is from right side, but the carry is extra-difficult because the golfer on the tee cannot see the far side of the hazard.

#17 ST. ANDREWS—OLD COURSE.
461 YARDS   PAR 4

shot, though out of vogue in recent years because of safety concerns. While safety must be considered, I think the rare blind shot adds interest to the course, because it adds variety and because so many players are uncomfortable with it. Any Scotsman will tell you that a hole is blind only once, after which you will know where to play; and when you swing the club you're looking at your ball anyway, not the target.

No doubt my fondness for the occasional blind shot was developed by my association with Pete Dye, by acclamation the master of psychological design among modern golf architects. In recent years Pete has made a point of building short par-4 holes featuring blind or semiblind half-wedge approach shots, simply because these were the shots the Tour pros complained about the most as being unfair on the TPC at Sawgrass and at PGA West.

Dye has taken the tournament players' interest in design and used it against them: Employing design tactics which irritate them, he distracts them from their real purpose, to play the course in the fewest strokes. The other half of his logic is that an average player isn't worried about such esoteric questions of fair design, and consequently isn't distracted, giving him a competitive chance.

Golf architects understand this mental trap all too well; it disturbs their own golf games. When they see a hole they think is poorly designed, they become distracted, and play it poorly as a result. While it is hoped that those who read this book will be enlightened in the mysteries of design, they are forewarned to reserve their criticisms of the course until the 19th hole, lest they fall into the same trap.

6

DESIGN
AND THE PLAYER

*"The strategy of the golf course is the soul of the game.
The spirit of golf is to dare a hazard, and by negotiating
it reap a reward, while he who fears or declines the issue
of the carry, has a longer or harder shot for his second; yet
the player who avoids the unwise effort gains advantage
over one who tries for more than in him lies, or who fails
under the test."*
—GEORGE THOMAS, Golf Architecture in America, 1927.

Architecture was an integral part of golf on the earliest
Scottish links. The greens were located on the best patches of
turf, but since there were no formalized fairways, it was up to
the players to "design" the best route to the hole while avoiding
the natural hazards. Ever since, the strategy of play has been
part of the interest of golf.

Modern golf architects of the past hundred years have
sought to re-create the strategic interest of the early links, with
varying degrees of success. In the process, three distinct styles
or schools of design have emerged: the penal, the strategic,
and the heroic.

THE THREE SCHOOLS OF GOLF DESIGN

The most simplistic approach to design, found on the earliest constructed courses, is to lay out hazards from the tee forward to the green, placing bunkers to punish a topped drive, a hook or a slice, or a wayward approach. Because the purpose of such hazards is to punish a poor shot, this style of design is referred to as the *penal* school of architecture. It should be noted, however, that a hole which is penal in concept may still have balanced shot values: Pine Valley, for example, features wide fairways and large greens. Gradually, thoughtful architects realized that the profusion of hazards had far greater effect on the beginning golfer than on the accomplished player, and penal design went out of vogue.

The greatest goal of golf architecture is to arrange a course difficult enough to hold the interest of the accomplished golfer, without so many hazards that the weaker player becomes discouraged.

Ever since the golden age of design in the early 1900's, the style of choice in golf course design has been the *strategic* school. The essence of this style is for the green to be heavily defended on one side or tilted significantly, so there is a distinct advantage to placing the drive in a certain part of the fairway. Fairway hazards are placed only to make the optimum lines of attacking the green risky. For example, a bunker may be placed at the front left of the green, and the green sloped away from the bunker to reward an approach from the right; another bunker is placed to the right of the fairway, just where the expert would try to drive to set up the easiest approach to the green. The golfer's approach must therefore be similar to the strategy of pocket billiards: The expert player seeks not only to make progress with each shot, but to position his ball so that his subsequent shots will easily follow. The motto of the strategic school comes from a description once written of Woking Golf Club, England: "No money or labour is wasted

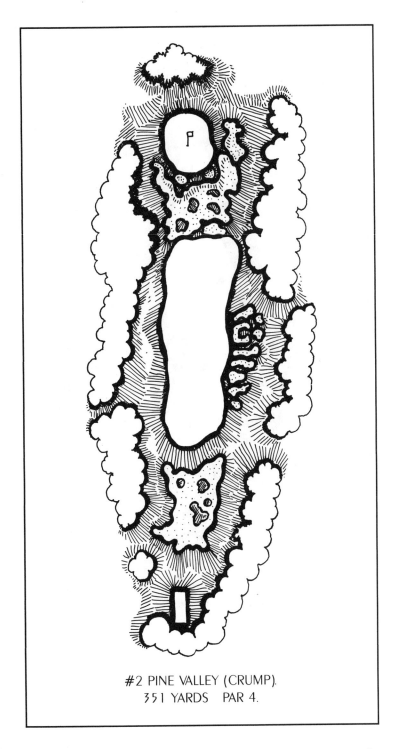

#2 PINE VALLEY (CRUMP).
351 YARDS   PAR 4.

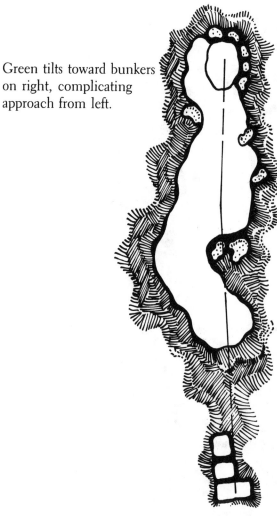

Green tilts toward bunkers
on right, complicating
approach from left.

Added bunkers keep long
hitter honest.

Bunkers must be carried
on drive for best angle of
approach.

#3 SUNNINGDALE—OLD (PARK).
296 YARDS   PAR 4.

68

in needless endeavour to emphasise the infirmity of the congenitally feeble and inaccurate."

The *heroic* school of design is an offshoot of the strategic: A clear advantage is gained on the approach by making a significant carry from the tee. The ideal form of heroic hazard is the one laid out on a diagonal, so that every player has the thrill of carrying their own requisite portion of hazard. Yet such hazards seldom trap the Tour-caliber golfer, who judges how far he can safely carry the ball, and hedges to the side of safety so that even his miss-hit will safely clear the hazard. The hazard with an irregular edge provides great food for thought, especially for the player who hits his drive just the distance where a choice must be made between attempting the dangerous carry, or playing more safely than he would like.

Both the heroic and the strategic schools require the golfer to weigh the risks of the driving hazard against the advantage of position for his subsequent shots to the green. He must think out his attack from the green backwards, based on an honest assessment of his own abilities. In contrast, the essence of the penal school is that there are no real options: he must hit a straight tee shot between hazards (although he might use a shorter club off the tee, sacrificing length for control), or deal with the consequences.

In applying these labels, it is crucial to distinguish between the penal *school* and the penal *hazard*. The arrangement of the bunkers, rather than their individual difficulty, defines the three schools. A hole with a deep pot bunker right in the middle of the fairway is of the strategic school, if the fairway is sufficiently wide to give the golfer options on his drive. A hole with a wide fairway and shallow bunkers to either side of the landing area is of the penal school, unless there is great advantage to be gained by placing the tee shot to one side of the fairway instead of down the middle.

Difficult hazards, which the golfer may label penal, are the essence of interesting golf, and nowhere more so than in the *strategic* school, where there ought to be a distinct penalty for

Green runs away from middle to back, subtly penalizing longer approach shots.

Fairway widens at left so a "safe" drive won't run through into rough

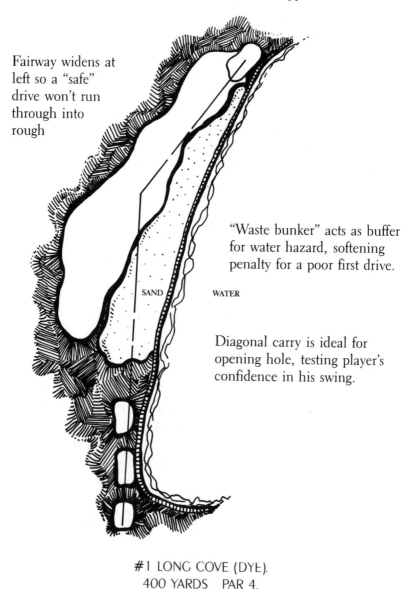

"Waste bunker" acts as buffer for water hazard, softening penalty for a poor first drive.

SAND   WATER

Diagonal carry is ideal for opening hole, testing player's confidence in his swing.

#1 LONG COVE (DYE).
400 YARDS   PAR 4.

the golfer who has failed to heed the hazard after being given plenty of room to do so. We might go so far as to say that the strategically arranged hole should feature the most difficult or penal hazards, whereas the penally arranged hole must not have penal hazards if it is to remain playable for the average golfer.

From the standpoint of semantics, all architects would prefer to be identified as members of the strategic school of design. Yet the best golf courses are those which borrow from all three schools.[1] No course adheres completely to the noble maxims of strategic design, for three reasons. First is the cost. The totally strategic course would require an enormous acreage of fairway if the average player was to be given latitude to avoid the hazards. Second is that the purely strategic hole can become somewhat boring to the average golfer consistently falling short of its driving hazards. Finally, the occasional heroic or penal hole will add variety to the course, and will confront the golfer with psychological tension of particular value to the golfer playing by himself, or in situations when one man has gone well up in a stroke competition and would avoid all risks to preserve his lead.

Some players have vilified the deep fairway pot bunkers found on the links and on some early American courses for being penal and unfair, and insist that a fairway bunker be shallow enough to give them a chance to reach the green with a heroic recovery. Yet the value of severe hazards is to reinforce the role of proper strategy, to see whether the player will admit his mistake or try to save the stroke and risk compounding his error.

Perhaps the ultimate example of the value of fairway pot bunkers was the play of Bobby Clampett on the 42nd (6th)

[1]To cite one famous example, the Amen Corner at Augusta National features one purely strategic hole, the par-4 11th; one essentially penal hole, the famous par-3 12th, where there is no real option but to hit the ball between Rae's Creek and the back bunkers; and a classic heroic hole, the short par-5 13th.

"Gate" of fairway bunkers for long hitter's second shot; length of hole makes it difficult enough for short hitter without added bunkers.

Second pot bunker is primary hazard when downwind, and adds to penal value of first bunker.

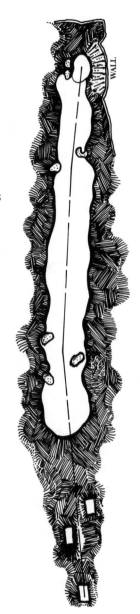

#6 ROYAL TROON—OLD.
577 YARDS   PAR 5.

hole of the 1982 British Open at Royal Troon, when he was leading the field by eight clear shots. After driving into a pot bunker on the long par-5, he attempted to escape with an 8-iron in order to get within reach of the green and preserve one stroke. His shot caught the lip of the bunker and was deflected into another close by. Again, he chose a 9-iron to try and make up lost ground, but the shot caught the lip of the bunker and advanced only about fifty yards. Lying three, he tried to reach the green with a 3-wood even though it was now pretty much out of range, and hooked the ball wide of the green into the deep rough. From there, he could have pitched safely to the center of the green and taken two putts for his double bogey. Instead, he tried to cut his fifth shot just over the pot bunker next to the green, fell short, and wound up with a triple bogey 8. His confidence destroyed, he never made another birdie for the remainder of the tournament, playing the final two rounds in 155 strokes after taking 133 for the first two.

Many modern architects build shallow fairway bunkers, with little hazard value, simply to avoid the penal tag, and to make their holes difficult enough to be interesting resort to a penal arrangement of bunkering.

Another point of dispute concerns how simple or complex the strategy of the hole should be. Robert Trent Jones, for one, has stated in no uncertain terms that "the line of play should be obvious from the tee." The holes fulfilling this ideal are the penal holes, where there is only one safe route to be found.

The paradox of strategic design is that the simplest golf holes produce the most interesting play. The most interesting tee shot is not the one which provides two options—black or white—but the one presenting a clear hazard (black) and 100 shades of grey to the side of it, forcing the golfer to weigh how much risk he is willing to take against how much margin for error he needs. A perfect example is the par-4 12th hole at North Berwick, Scotland. Its green tilts sharply from right to left, so the ideal approach is from the inside corner of the dogleg, defended by a single, small, deep pot bunker. It is easy

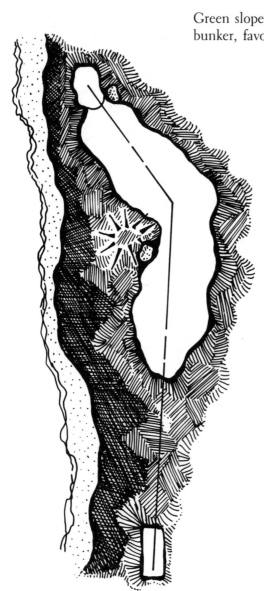

Green slopes right-to-left away from bunker, favoring approach from left.

Plenty of room to right of bunker, but gives longer approach.

Pot bunker set into dune at 230 yards from tee. Short driver may play to left for best angle into green, but dune obscures good view of green.

#12 NORTH BERWICK—WEST LINKS.
373 YARDS   PAR 4.

to imagine the local citizen giving this penal bunker a wide berth at first, and progressively playing closer to it on each subsequent round, until one day a pull into the bunker yields a double bogey, and the next day the process starts all over again.

By contrast, the complicated designs of modern architects often leave the player with obvious choices, essentially no choice at all. One of the clearest examples is the hole with alternate fairways, where the player must decide from the tee which of two routes to take. The problem with this plan is that one route is usually the clear favorite, but it demands a long carry from the tee. The long hitters nearly always take the shortcut, and the short hitters will have no choice but to go around. Instead, the shorter route should emphasize a straight shot, so that everyone has the choice of taking either option.

The unsung advantage of the strategic and heroic schools of design over the penal school is the added interest in competitive play. On a penal hole, there is no choice but to play for the fairway and play for the green, and hope to hit the ball straight; such a hole might be well suited to the end of the course, so that a golfer with a clear lead cannot play three conservative iron shots to avoid all the hazards. But on a strategic hole, the golfer is confronted with optional routes, and forced to make his decisions in the context of both his abilities and the standing of his opponent. If there is a diagonal carry off the tee and his opponent has already found the hazard, surely the golfer will hedge toward safety so as not to immediately give back his advantage. But if his opponent hits a brilliant recovery, the conservative tee shot might wind up costing him the hole.

Another aspect of strategic design is that instead of simply rewarding the player who hits the ball farthest or straightest, it gives the advantage to the golfer who honestly accepts the strengths and limitations of his own game. In the example just cited, the man who can carry the farther part of the hazard gains the advantage, but if he overestimates his ability he will

Green presents extremely shallow target from left-hand fairway, with modest grass bunkers to catch shots that do not hold; but short hitters must still make two forced carries.

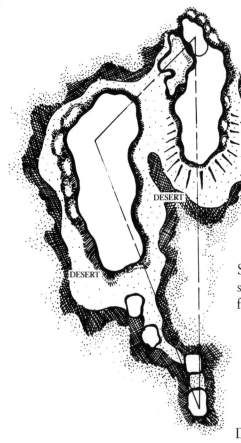

Short-cut fairway is built up starkly at front, while left-hand fairway is more inviting.

Difficult-to-arrange forward tees—must minimize carry to "easy" fairway, thus tampering with alignment for direct route.

#13 DESERT HIGHLANDS (NICKLAUS).
396 YARDS   PAR 4.

wind up at a disadvantage against a shorter-hitting opponent who plays within himself.

On the best championship courses, such decisions have to be made on virtually every shot—even around the greens, if they are properly and interestingly contoured. Should I chip from off the green, or lag up close to the hole with the "Texas wedge"? Should I take a run at this ten-foot downhill putt, or can I afford to leave myself a four-footer coming back if I miss? Golf strategy comes in all shapes and sizes.

SHOTMAKING: THE LOST ART

An alternative concept of architecture is to reward the player not just for hitting long and straight, or for correctly planning his attack, but for his ability to control the flight of the ball through swing technique. This was an important component of golf in the early days, because golf links in Britain were not designed for the playing of specific shots. The holes were cut in "sporting" locations by the players, and it was up to them to get the ball close to the hole with whatever sort of stroke served the purpose. The inventive player who could play the widest variety of tricky approaches was the champion of the early days.

The science of golf may have come a long way in the last 100 years, but in many respects, these "improvements" have taken away from the art of shotmaking. Golf courses have become relatively standardized in their demands and hazards, and the science of golf course maintenance has advanced to the point that the golfer seldom encounters a bad lie in the fairway or bunker, or a bad bounce on his approach. Clubs and balls have been scientifically designed to help correct the average golfer's hooks and slices, making it more difficult for the skilled golfer to deliberately play these same shots. The modern champion has perfected his swing full-throttle on the practice range, knows the yardages and the true distance value of each of his clubs, and repeats the same swing with machinelike precision with every club in his bag.

The few real shotmakers found in golf today, such as Trevino, Ballesteros, and Chi Chi Rodriguez, are probably the last of a dying breed, because there isn't much need for shotmaking on modern courses.

While all other factors are working to eliminate the art of shotmaking from the game, I believe it should be the highest aspiration of the golf architect to design holes giving the greatest scope for the shotmaker's skills. His credo should be as John Low professed in 1903:

> "Every fresh hole we play should teach us some new possibility of using our strokes and suggest to us a further step in the progress of our golfing knowledge."
> —JOHN LOW, *Concerning Golf*, 1903.

Modern golf architecture has fallen woefully short of Low's ideal. But there are golf holes still in existence that reward the shotmaker's special talents, and I would like to concentrate on these for the remainder of this chapter.

I must emphasize that while holes can be designed to reward shotmaking skill, playing conditions—the wind and the firmness of the ground—can accomplish the same thing. In regions where the wind does blow, its intensity adds an urgency to nearly every shot, for it affects either the distance value of the shot or its flight pattern, and it forces the golfer to allow for this effect. The expert player, on the other hand, devises a way to use the wind to his advantage: He may hit a high ball downwind, work the ball with the wind to gain extra distance, or work the ball into a side wind so it will stop quickly.

One paradoxical effect of the wind on British links is that it can make short shots more difficult than longer ones. The standard play on the Postage Stamp 8th hole at Royal Troon would be a high nine-iron shot, but when the wind is howling, its effect on the high-flying shot is impossible to judge. The golfer is compelled to produce a low, punched three-quarter shot on such a hole, a difficult prospect when the green is small and well-guarded.

Another shot called for on the links is the approach that bounces short of the green and rolls forward to the hole, a necessity if the ground is hard and there is not much forward tilt of the green to help stop the ball. When soggy conditions prevail, the standard aerial approach stops so quickly that a good player is never tempted to play a trickier shot to get close to the hole. When the ground is firm, the golfer must be able to control not only how far his shot is going to fly, but what it is going to do once it lands. This is the shotmaker's realm.

In warmer climates, a simple step toward firm conditions would be to stop the practice of overseeding in winter. Dormant Bermuda fairways make for a fine playing surface and require no irrigation when in hibernation. On northern courses, irrigation could be reduced in many places from an everyday practice to an occasional supplement, and there should be more experiments with fescues and buffalograss on the fairways where conditions are favorable.

Many links feature greens laid across the ground in a spot where they are flat or fall slightly away from the line of the shot, and on firm ground this shot is no easier to judge with a short iron approach than with a wooden club, which is why the links have maintained their challenge in the face of modern improvements in equipment. Garden City Golf Club is one of few American courses featuring the fall-away green prominently.

A variation of the same principle is the green sharply tilted from side to side, exemplified by the short par-4 10th hole at Riviera, or the longer 5th hole at Merion. In both cases the slope of the green is so severe from right to left that an approach hooked into the green will almost certainly release and roll off the green on the left. The only approach is a fade finishing below the hole. But at Riviera the bulk of the fairway is to the right of the axis of the green and the green almost within reach

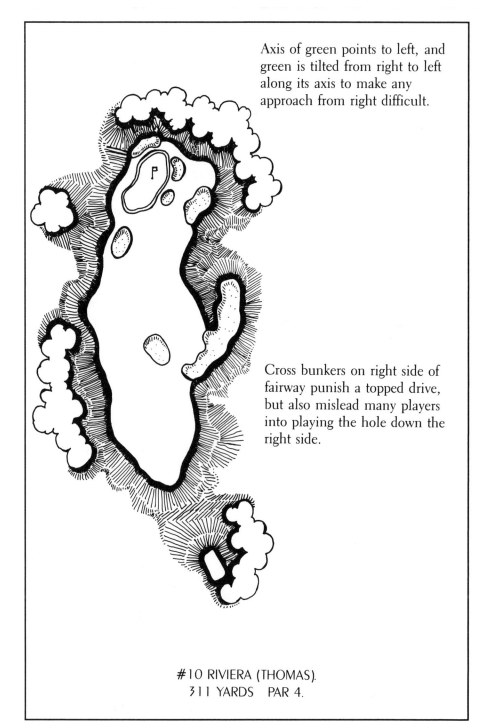

Axis of green points to left, and green is tilted from right to left along its axis to make any approach from right difficult.

Cross bunkers on right side of fairway punish a topped drive, but also mislead many players into playing the hole down the right side.

#10 RIVIERA (THOMAS).
311 YARDS   PAR 4.

80

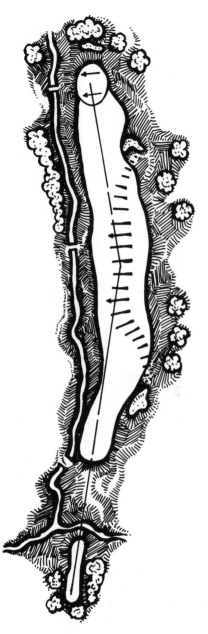

Green tilts sharply from right to left; difficult to hold with shot from right of fairway.

Long driver must aim very near line of stream to keep on low side of fairway for best approach. Fairway tilts from right toward stream.

#5 MERION—EAST (HUGH WILSON).
426 YARDS   PAR 4.

from the tee, luring the golfer away from the best approach line. At Merion the fairway tilts sharply from right to left; the stance makes it is difficult to play a fade except from the low side of the fairway, which is closely guarded by a narrow brook.

Another such hole is the dogleg 4th at Myopia near Boston, the site of four U.S. Opens at the turn of the century. In the old days, its 392 yards required a long approach for the best players, played in the same manner that the club member must approach the hole today: a low draw to the right-hand entrance of the green, judged to lose speed at just the right moment, then to turn sharply left down the slope of the green. But the same tilt of the green has given the hole a fine defense against today's long hitter: It is so sharp that he must beware his standard high approach spinning back down off the front left of the green. He must try to place his tee shot near the corner of the dogleg and fade his second shot up against the slope of the green if it is to stop predictably.

The ingenious designer may occasionally create a long hole where judgment of approach is more important than length of tee shot. My own 3rd hole at High Pointe is the best I have so designed to date. The small green is perched on a knob well above a valley of fairway, with almost-level ground mowed at fairway height to the left of the putting surface, but with a fairly steep fall both in front of and behind the green. For the short hitter, the incline at the front of the green is little problem; his long iron or fairway wood approach will readily climb it, but since he is unlikely to consistently hit such a small target from so far away, he typically plays a fade at the left-hand edge of the green to give himself the easiest chip if the shot does not come off. The player who has hit a long drive does not have it much easier. If his short-iron approach is short it will likely not bounce up onto the green, and the crowned green is quite small to hit and hold without going over and down the hill in back. The hole gives the greatest champion a chance to show his full arsenal of shots, but for most players it is a question of a four or a

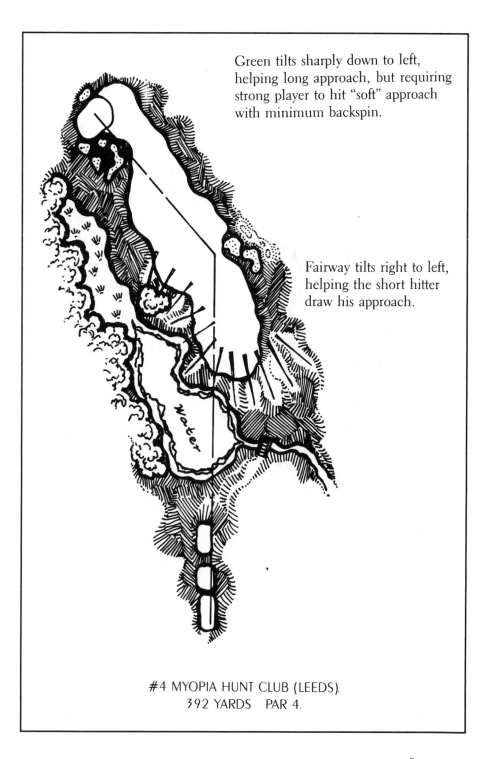

Green tilts sharply down to left, helping long approach, but requiring strong player to hit "soft" approach with minimum backspin.

Fairway tilts right to left, helping the short hitter draw his approach.

Water

#4 MYOPIA HUNT CLUB (LEEDS).
392 YARDS   PAR 4.

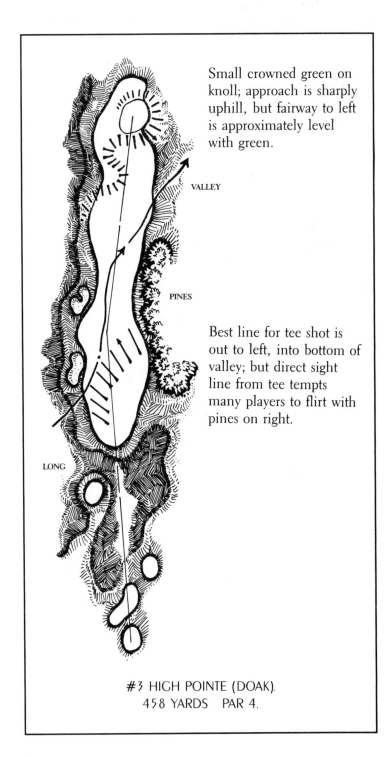

Small crowned green on knoll; approach is sharply uphill, but fairway to left is approximately level with green.

VALLEY

PINES

Best line for tee shot is out to left, into bottom of valley; but direct sight line from tee tempts many players to flirt with pines on right.

LONG

#3 HIGH POINTE (DOAK).
458 YARDS   PAR 4.

five, and the short hitter often has as much chance of saving his par as the stronger man.

Other times a hole will reward shotmaking skill not by giving the player the option between two different kinds of shots, but by forcing him to choose between trying to make a specific shot or laying up. On such a hole, an advantage should be gained by the golfer executing the requisite shot, but ideally the golfer who admits his weakness should be rewarded for his discretion. A good example is the 2nd hole at The Dunes Golf & Beach Club in Myrtle Beach. Trees on the left off the tee and a quick dogleg allow a tee shot of only 220 yards, unless the golfer can produce a controlled draw off the tee, a tough assignment so early in the round. The player who brings off the shot is rewarded with a short-iron approach, but the hole is of a length that the golfer safely laying up to the corner can get home with a long second; the golfer who hooks into the trees surely cannot.

The tee shots at both the 10th and 13th holes at Augusta National employ the hilly contours of the site to give a distinct advantage to a hooked tee shot. At the 10th, a properly hooked ball catches a severe slope in the fairway and runs well down the hill to the left, while a straight tee shot stays on the higher ground, leaving a much longer approach from a tougher angle. At the 13th, both the azaleas and Rae's Creek encroach upon the ideal driving line along the left. Only a hooked tee ball can fly around the corner of the dogleg and find a relatively flat lie for the second shot. In both instances, the shot values of Augusta are more exacting than that of the 2nd hole at The Dunes, as befits a championship course. Both holes are of such a length that the player who does not produce a hook from the tee will have to strain to get home with his second shot.

Finally, there are occasionally good holes where only one type of approach shot will get the ball within reasonable distance of a birdie putt. In fairness, I believe such holes should be used sparingly, for two reasons. The first reason is philosophical: It is the point of golf architecture not to *dictate* to the golfer how a hole should be played, but to create a situation where the

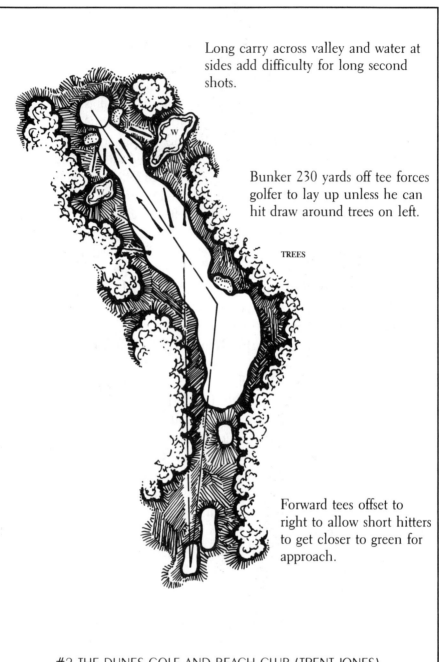

Long carry across valley and water at sides add difficulty for long second shots.

Bunker 230 yards off tee forces golfer to lay up unless he can hit draw around trees on left.

TREES

Forward tees offset to right to allow short hitters to get closer to green for approach.

#2 THE DUNES GOLF AND BEACH CLUB (TRENT JONES).
422 YARDS   PAR 4.

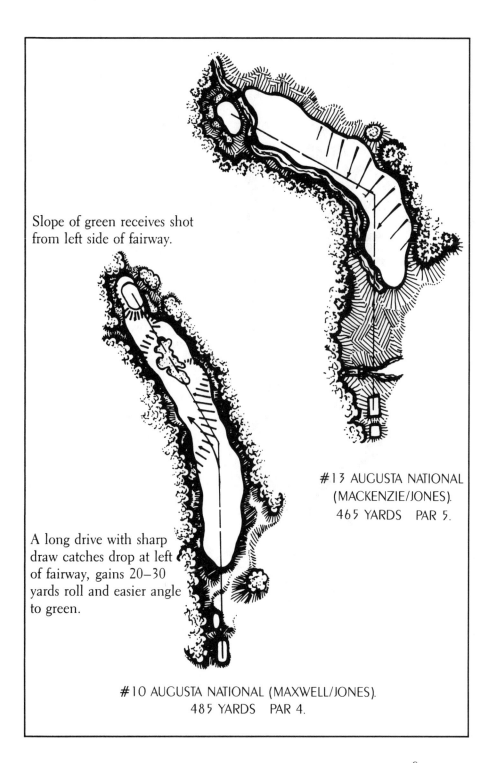

Slope of green receives shot from left side of fairway.

#13 AUGUSTA NATIONAL (MACKENZIE/JONES). 465 YARDS   PAR 5.

A long drive with sharp draw catches drop at left of fairway, gains 20–30 yards roll and easier angle to green.

#10 AUGUSTA NATIONAL (MAXWELL/JONES). 485 YARDS   PAR 4.

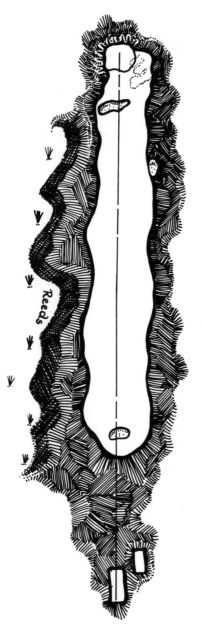

Green is too shallow to hold a long approach, but low rolls at entrance help steer running approach up onto green.

Reeds

Lack of fairway hazards encourage a straightaway drive, but contours on approach favor second shot from right.

#9 WESTWARD HO!
482 YARDS   PAR 5.

player's ingenuity can be exercised. There is much more to admire when the idea for the shot is the player's rather than the architect's. For this reason, an architect hates to have to explain his holes to frustrated players unable to figure out the best method of attack. Sometimes even I cannot figure out the best way to attack one of my holes until I have played it several times. That's when I know I have hit upon something really interesting.

The second reason is more practical. If playing conditions are severe, then there may be times when the one shot the hole was designed around will not work, and the hole is impossible to play. A hole with a long forced carry over water to a shallow green is a common design failure. What is the player to do when a gale is blowing from behind, or his drive has unluckily found a lie in a divot scrape? The same holds true for a forced carry from the tee when a gale is blowing into the player's face, or for a sharply canted green designed to receive a run-up shot after ten straight days of rain (although in the latter case it is difficult to imagine a green so severe that the ball could not be pitched near the hole under soggy conditions).

The type of holes where a "tricky" approach is most often acceptable are the between-length holes: a very long par-3, a driveable par-4, a long par-4, or a short par-5. The strong player would otherwise have an almost insurmountable advantage over the short hitter. In such a situation, it is arguable that the stronger player should have to show unusual skill as well as strength if he is to take the hole easily.

One of the finest examples of such a hole is the short par-5 9th at Westward Ho! in southwestern England. It still plays as it was described in 1910:

> "The ninth green lies in a hollow on the top of a small plateau at the range of two very full shots from the tee, and the superlative virtue of the hole consists in a little unobtrusive pot-bunker in the face of the hill. We can hardly hope to drive far enough to carry the bunker in our second, and if we could it would scarcely be possible to stay on the green. Therefore, we must drive well out

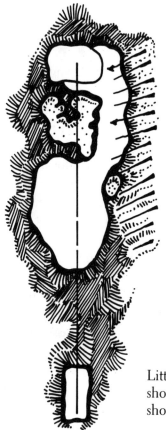

Short hitter may use slope at right to kick ball down to edge of green, but must carry small bunker or fade around it, restricting bounce to left.

Little differential between tees; shortest hitters must lay up short of bunker.

#4 RIVIERA (THOMAS).
238 YARDS   PAR 3.

to the right, and hope to reach the green with a subtle
hook. The ground breaks in toward the hole from the
right, and so a perfectly played shot, with just sufficient
hook, will keep turning and turning towards the hole, till
it totters with its last gasp down the last slope and lies
close to the hole. Often, of course, it will be out of the
question to get home in two, but the hole will still be
interesting, and our approach shot anything but a simple one."

—BERNARD DARWIN, *The Golf Courses*
of the British Isles, 1910.

The same type of shot can be designed into a long par-3 hole.
The 4th at Riviera is just such a hole, although the bunker
guarding the green is a hundred times as large. Even the famous
Redan, in spite of the big green that allows scope for alternate
methods of play, rewards the same type of approach shot.

Most every British links features at least one long hole with a
very tricky approach, although we often find that the same hole
called a short par-5 at the turn of the century is now considered
a long par-4. (Ironically, the fact that these holes are now
somewhat easier to reach in two makes them more controversial, simply because the par has changed on the scorecard.) The
Road hole at St. Andrews is the most well-known example of
such a hole, but two others that come to mind are the 14th at
Royal Dornoch, known as "Foxy," and the 13th at Prestwick,
the "Sea Headrig" hole. The two holes have only one bunker
between them, but in each case the green is set at an odd angle
to the fairway and requires a special degree of shotmaking to
land the ball short of the green and get it to bounce up and stay
on. The 14th at Royal Dornoch is a high plateau green too
shallow to hit and hold with a long iron, while the 13th at
Prestwick angles off to the right behind a low hummock of
fairway which either stops an approach shot dead or sends it
skittering over the green. By the same token, both greens make
for supremely interesting short play, rewarding every yard the
short hitter can muster with his first two shots. In both cases,
too, it is noteworthy that the golfer who goes for the green with

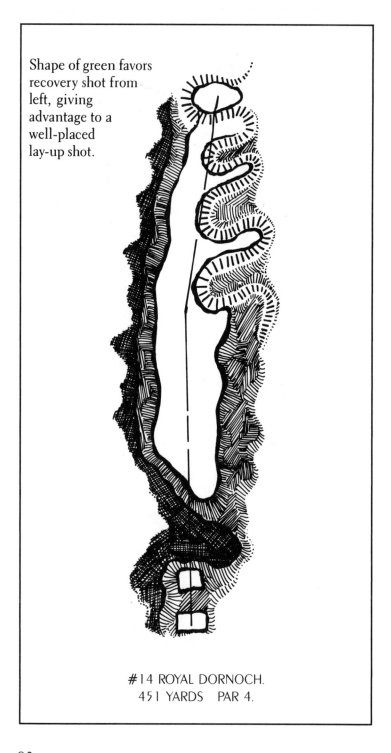

Shape of green favors
recovery shot from
left, giving
advantage to a
well-placed
lay-up shot.

#14 ROYAL DORNOCH.
451 YARDS   PAR 4.

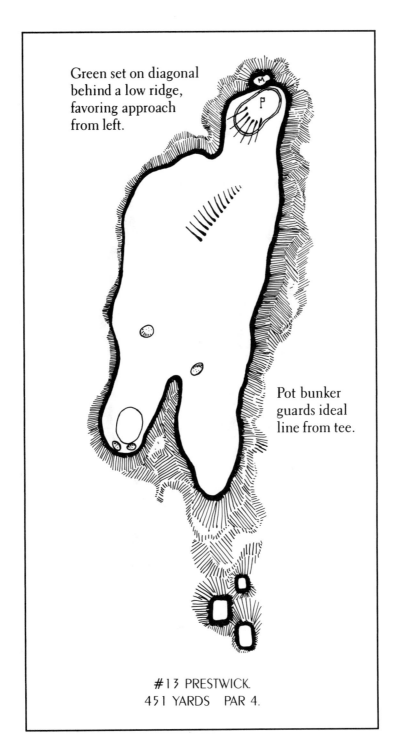

Green set on diagonal
behind a low ridge,
favoring approach
from left.

Pot bunker
guards ideal
line from tee.

#13 PRESTWICK.
451 YARDS   PAR 4.

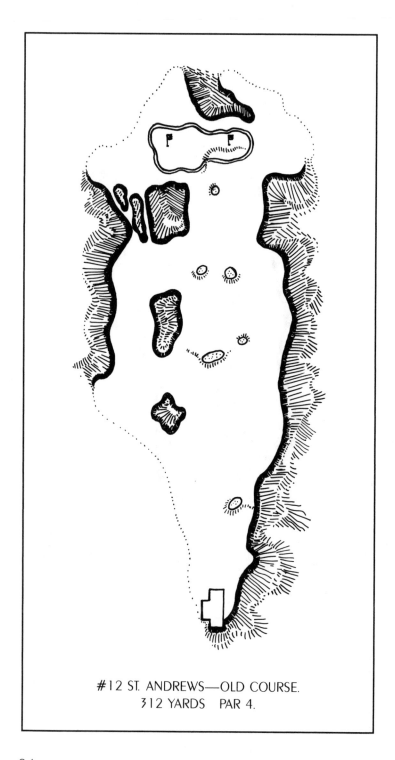

#12 ST. ANDREWS—OLD COURSE.
312 YARDS   PAR 4.

his second, and falls short to the right, leaves himself a much tougher pitch than the golfer who admitted he could not make it and played to the left for the best angle into the green for his third shot.

The 12th on the Old Course at St. Andrews also requires an unusual approach. It is a short two-shotter that features a shallow shelf of green only twelve paces deep, with lower levels both in front and behind. There is no room to land and stop the ball on the higher level; even the best shots bounce once before spinning back to the hole, and the first bounce would likely take the ball to the lower level in back of the green. The standard plan of attack is to drive as close to the green as one can, flirting with a handful of unseen fairway bunkers in the process. If this is safely accomplished, the ideal approach shot is a short running ball clambering up the tier in the green and coming to a stop.

Shotmaking can also be called into play in the short game. The same contours that create an interesting approach will also cause havoc for recovery shots, especially where they are mowed as fairway so the golfer does not necessarily have to pitch back to the green on the fly. The most original example is the famous "Dell Hole" at Lahinch in Ireland, a blind par-3 hole to a shallow green wedged between massive sandhills. The hole is often villified as nothing more than a matter of luck, since there is only a marker stone on the hill in front of the green to indicate the location of the hole, and often both short and long shots sometimes bounce off the sandhills and come down onto the green. But the same hills provide scope for fascinating "carom-shot" recoveries for the smart player who has missed the green, as I discovered one day while observing play.

Holes like these are rare or nonexistent on modern courses, but the game would be much more interesting and fun if there were more. As Robert Hunter concluded in *The Links*, "Great golfers would find the game stupid if no occasion arose to use the most difficult shots in their repertoire."

7

THE GREEN
COMPLEX

*"Putting greens are to golf courses what faces are to
portraits."*
—CHARLES BLAIR MACDONALD, Scotland's Gift - Golf.

As a golfer becomes proficient at the game, the greens of
the golf course take on great importance in his total score. In a
perfectly played par round, half the strokes will be putts, and
the ability to get approach shots or chip shots close to the pin
will depend on the contours and firmness of the green. Therefore better players place enormous emphasis on the design and
maintenance of the greens in their evaluation of any course.

Proper green design concerns two separate but interlocking
issues: how the green complex (including surrounding hazards) affects approach play, and how the surface of the green
presents difficulties in putting. The two aspects of design are

accomplished at once, of course—the contours of the green and its surrounds should seamlessly blend together so that the green is not an obvious artifice in the landscape. But for organizational purposes, I will tackle the two subjects separately.

On flat ground, the architect might conceive the contours of his green first, and design outward from there. But on good property, he is likely to use the natural contours around the green site as the foundation of his design, add bunkers accordingly, and then work inward to the contours of the green itself.

The design of the green complex thus goes back to the choice of site. On good property, many of the greens can be located in spots with inherent interest. A natural plateau or ridge, a slight knoll, or a punch bowl that is well-drained present inherent problems to which the golf architect may add.

On many modern courses, the surface of the green is sloped toward the fairway to aid the player in stopping his approach shot, but this is not necessarily the rule. A flat or slightly back-sloping green site has instant merit because of the difficulty in stopping an approach shot. It is one of the few situations where the difficulty of the shot stands the test of time, because a short approach shot does not make things much easier. This is one reason why St. Andrews and other Scottish links, laid out on flattish ground, can be so interesting.

The architect's first step is to determine the size and shape of the green. While these are mostly a factor of the architect's strategy for each hole, there is also a minimum-size requirement, which depends on the volume of play the course must bear. The green must be large enough that the hole can be moved to spread out the traffic, so that the grass does not become worn or the soil compacted around the hole.

There is no absolute rule of thumb for determining the minimum size of a green. It depends on many factors: the wear tolerance of the grass, the maintenance budget available, and ultimately the standard the players demand. While I cannot provide a simple formula to follow, I can make a few recommendations based on well-known courses.

Northern championship courses such as Winged Foot and Inverness (averaging 25,000 to 30,000 rounds of golf per year) get by with greens averaging 4,000 square feet, but only with costly maintenance practices such as walk-mowing greens and frequent aeration. A southern course which will see heavy traffic for twelve months of the year (50,000 rounds) will rarely survive with less than 5,000 square feet of putting surface per hole.

Any single green of less than 3,000 square feet is likely to cause problems. In theory, small greens are the ultimate reward for precise iron play; but famous examples, such as the 7th at Pebble Beach and the small greens of Harbour Town, are almost always in poor shape due to the amount of traffic they receive. A green this size might be satisfactory for a private club playing 25,000 rounds or less, but it will always be a maintenance headache, so the designer should use such features advisedly.

As the minimum workable size for a green is based on wear in the area around the hole, a green of exaggerated contour or shape has to be of good size. Every green loses a certain amount of pin-placement area because the hole is never located within ten or fifteen feet of the edge of the green, but a heavily contoured green may have other unusable areas because the hole cannot be located on a severe slope. Narrow tongues of green are also wasted space, because the hole has to be located well away from the two edges.

When in doubt as to sufficient area for a green, it is always better to err on the large side during construction, even though it may be costly. A green can always be mowed smaller to reduce annual upkeep while business is slow, but it can never be enlarged beyond the prepared soil while maintaining quality. Good courses eventually become popular, and it is wise to allow for growth.

Many people believe that in the name of equity, the size of the green should be in direct proportion to the length of the

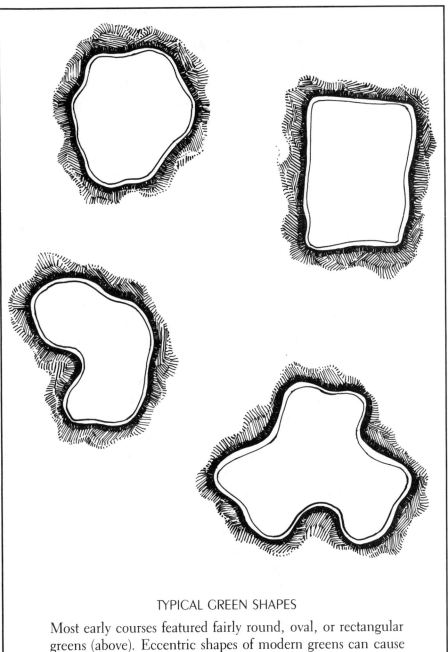

TYPICAL GREEN SHAPES

Most early courses featured fairly round, oval, or rectangular greens (above). Eccentric shapes of modern greens can cause problems; if such greens are flat, it may be impossible to aim the first putt on a makeable line.

expected approach shot, but this would only be true if we had to make every hole of equal difficulty. Often, great holes go directly against this simplistic definition of shot values.

For example, the 2nd hole at Pine Valley is a short par-4 with a very large green. The green needs to be big considering the severity of the surrounding hazards and the forced-carry approach. It is also severely contoured to ensure that a loose approach shot will still lead to trouble. At the other end of the spectrum, the Road hole at St. Andrews has an extremely long approach shot to an extremely narrow target. It is intended to be a severe hole for the good player, and the green is just the right size to present an interesting third shot to the majority of players not home in two. Were the green big enough to be "fair" for the professional's approach, the short hitter would have a boring 2nd shot and a boring pitch to play.

The relationship which matters most is not the size of the green versus the length of the approach, but *the size of the hazard-free area around the hole versus the difficulty level of the approach*. If this is properly balanced, then the course will remain fair for all players, and more interesting to boot.

One of my least favorite trends in modern design is the unusually shaped green. On nearly all classic courses the greens have a fairly simple oval or pear shape; the line which describes the circumference is no perfect curve, by any means, but it rarely bows away from the center of the green. Any time it does so, there is the possibility that a player whose ball rests on the very edge of the green might not be able to putt straight for a hole cut near the same edge, because the collar or rough around the green is in his way. This leaves the player the equally unpleasant options of aiming his first putt to finish well away from the hole, putting through the fringe or rough, or chipping his ball off the putting surface. Since it is ordinarily a fluke whenever a player will come across this situation—he is usually too far away on his previous shot to account for it, and a difference of a couple of feet would mean he was chipping from the collar—this objectionable situation should be avoided at all costs.

There are examples of eccentrically shaped greens on classic courses, but they are few and far between: the hourglass 17th at Pebble Beach, the boomerang-shaped 7th at Crystal Downs, or the 6th at Riviera, with a bunker actually inside the confines of the putting surface. The first two greens are unusually contoured, however, so that an ingeniously played putt can be steered around the curve in the green. As for the 6th at Riviera, legend has it that Billy Casper once took a couple of big divots out of the green with practice swings, before playing his ball over the bunker with his wedge from one side of the green to the other—during a practice round for the upcoming tournament. He evidently disliked the concept even more than I do.

The most overlooked part of green design in modern golf architecture is the entrance to the green. The architect must visualize how a hole will be tackled by all levels of players, from beginner to expert. While it is difficult to imagine that a truly bad golfer could foresee a Tour professional's high, soft approach, modern architecture suggests that the reverse is also true: Some of our modern players-turned-architects need a refresher course in the trajectory of the average player's shots.[1]

Whatever the scratch golfer's approach, the average player is frequently compelled to play a long-iron or wooden-club approach—a low shot which would have virtually no chance of staying on the green even if it carried all the way on the fly. Because the long shot has to be given room to lose its momentum, there should almost always be an open approach through which it can bounce onto the green. Moreover, the opening

---

[1]As Dr. Mackenzie pointed out, "the possession of a vivid imagination, which is an absolute essential in obtaining success [as an architect], may prevent him attaining a position among the higher ranks of players. Everyone knows how fatal imagination is in playing the game. Let the fear of socketing once enter your head, and you promptly socket every shot afterwards."

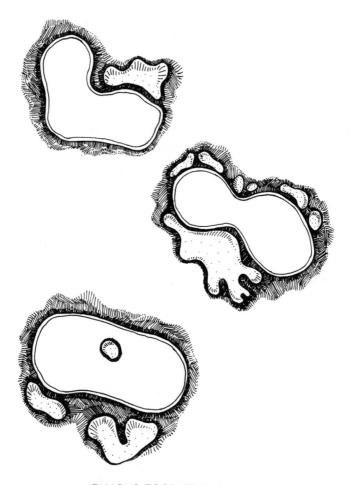

FAMOUS ECCENTRIC GREENS.
(TOP) #7 CRYSTAL DOWNS,
(MIDDLE) #17 PEBBLE BEACH,
(BOTTOM) #6 RIVIERA.

Despite these unusual shapes, there is rarely an impossible putt.
The seventh at Crystal Downs is banked up on the left at its bend,
so a ball can usually be putted around the curve from front to back.
The neck of the hourglass 17th at Pebble Beach is slightly
humpbacked, so with proper speed some extra break can be found.
The sixth at Riviera slopes sharply back left to front right, so a putt
can be worked at least partway around the interior bunker.

should *always* be mowed as fairway to give the golfer the benefit of the bounce. One of the most contrived situations in golf is the green, unguarded by hazards in front, whose approach is left as unmowed rough instead of fairway.

The island green completely closed off by hazards in front has a place on the course because of its do-or-die psychological interest, but it is best saved for holes that feature a very short approach shot, such as a par-3 under 150 yards or a par-4 of less than 350 yards. On any other hole, the average player should be given an entrance to aim for, or he will have no chance to take a risk to recover from a poor drive. He will be forced to lay up at the end of the fairway or to flail away for the green, knowing there is no chance the ball will stay on it even if he hits a great shot.

Old-time architects made specific recommendations as to the ideal width for the entrance to the green based on approach length, but it is really up to the individual's judgment. The entrance might be the entire width of the green on some holes; on others, it might be quite narrow, although below 30 feet in width it is for all practical purposes too narrow to aim at. On other occasions the entrance could be to one side of the green, forcing the short hitter to drive to a particular side of the fairway to be allowed the chance to bounce the ball on. If he misses his drive to the wrong side, he may play only for the apron of the green on the open side.

Many courses that once had carefully planned entrances have lost them over the years, because the superintendent did not realize their value and standardized the mowing of entrances to the greens to make them appear more formal. A narrow "neck" of fairway leading to the green is appropriate where there is a narrow opening between bunkers; where the opening is wider, it not only looks out of place to prepare a formal collar of rough at the entrance, but it may well defeat the architect's intention.

The location of the entrance can be complicated by undulations within the mowed area. Superintendents frequently

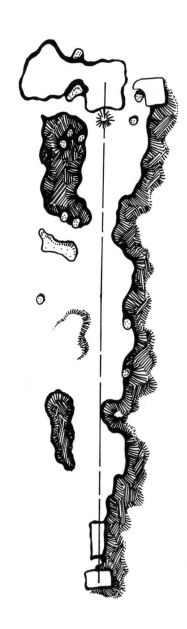

Deep bunker protects left-side pin placements, but mound in front comes more into play from right of fairway.

Mound, 4' high, lies just in front of green, deflecting long approaches, but giving little difficulty to short hitter's third shot.

#4 ST. ANDREWS—OLD COURSE.
464 YARDS   PAR 4.

Long, narrow green for
direct approach.

Hill at front left
will steer short
ball down to
green, but trees to
left stop long
hitter from bail-
ing out.

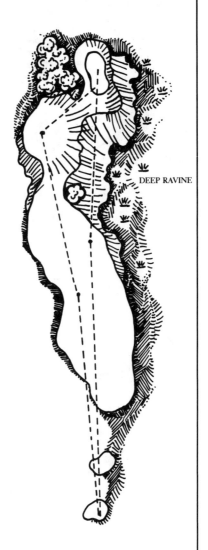

DEEP RAVINE

#16 LA CUMBRE (BRYCE).
416 YARDS   PAR 4.
(FROM GEORGE THOMAS,
GOLF ARCHITECTURE IN AMERICA, 1927.)

Steep bank behind green and slope of green reward shot below hole.

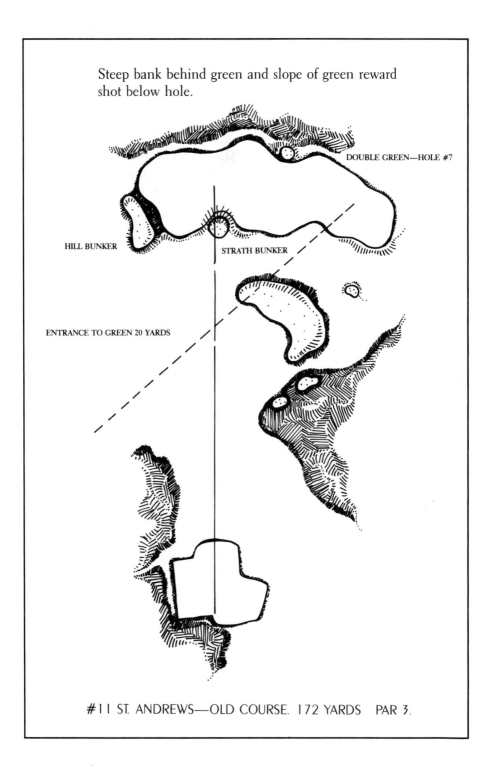

DOUBLE GREEN—HOLE #7

HILL BUNKER

STRATH BUNKER

ENTRANCE TO GREEN 20 YARDS

#11 ST. ANDREWS—OLD COURSE. 172 YARDS   PAR 3.

"define" the edges of the fairway by mowing around the base of such undulations, but they have much more effect on the game when mowed like fairway so the bounce is not smothered by long grass. For example, Pinehurst No. 2 and Royal Dornoch are well known for subtle crowns in front of the greens that steer all but the truly struck running approach away toward bunkers or swales at the sides of the green. The 4th hole on the Old Course at St. Andrews has a dramatic mound right in front of the green. When the fairways are firm in the summer and the greens are not holding well, the trick is to drive out to the very edge of the fairway and then to steer closely past the mound, without allowing it to turn away your approach. George Thomas built a hole at La Cumbre in California where the short hitter, just clearing a deep ravine, could play his ball into the side of a hill and let it totter down onto the front of a narrow green with the ravine along its right edge. Sadly, this hole has long since been subdued by a lenient green chairman.

No green, however, has a more perfectly fashioned entrance than the famed 11th hole at St. Andrews, the High Hole In. This green is defended on the right side by the deep Strath bunker, behind which the pin is usually placed on championship occasions. To the left the approach is open for some twenty yards. This entrance is just wide enough to lull the player into a sense of false security; if he aims safely away from Strath and pulls his iron shot slightly, he will surely find Hill bunker on the left of the green, where a 19-year-old Bob Jones picked up in self-disgust in the 1921 Open Championship.

GREENSIDE BUNKERS

Once the green has been located, the placement of the hazards depends mostly on the architect's strategy for the hole, but there are also maintenance considerations that apply, relating to foot traffic or maintenance equipment. Both sorts of traffic will eventually cause turf problems if the design does not address them.

Compaction from foot traffic around the hole is remedied by changing pin placements so that the most concentrated traffic occurs in a different spot each day. However, compaction will occur at the edge of the green if players all walk onto it from a single narrow path. The architect should take care to leave broad entrances to the green, especially from the cart path adjacent to the green. If the design dictates that bunkers should be between the cart path and the green, then either the bunkers should be broken up by grass walkways providing various access points, or the path should be relocated to the other side of the hole.

Compaction from maintenance equipment is minimized by mowing the green in a different direction each day: for example, lengthwise on Monday, crosswise on Tuesday, and diagonally on Wednesday. But where a hazard is located very close to the green, the mowing pattern must be interrupted to avoid it, and compaction may occur. Some designers in the 1950s, notably Robert Bruce Harris, went to the extreme of placing all their hazards at least one gang mower's width away from the collar of the green, to facilitate mowing. But the elimination of hazards close to the green may eliminate some strategic interest, and places the cart before the horse. Instead, the architect should simply be aware of such maintenance considerations and try to keep his transgressions to a few well-chosen places.

Within these guidelines, the two keys to the design of green complexes are variety and harmony. Each hole must have a character of its own, but still fit in to the overall style of the golf course.

Bunker placement around the greens is of the utmost importance, because the location of such hazards is the most visible and memorable part of the architect's work. In fact, considering the scratch golfer's proficiency at bunker play, the placement of bunkers around the green can almost now be approached as a visual exercise, because they have no more hazard value at the edge of a green than long rough.

Some architects of limited imagination place a bunker at each side of the green on hole after hole. But as we have explored in the chapter on psychology, by leaving one side of the green so it appears undefended, we induce golfers to miss the green to that side for safety, even though it may be more difficult for them to get up and down from the open side due to the contours of the green. The green without bunkers also has interest, because depth perception is hindered.

On other holes it is exciting to have the bunkers virtually surrounding the green. This works especially well on the par-3 holes, where little strategy is involved because all but the weakest players are aiming for the green; the memorable quality of the hole is confined to the beauty of the picture and the hazards around the green. Most modern architects seem unable to design a great par-3 hole without water, precisely because they are not building beautiful bunkers. Why not follow the prescription of John Low, who wrote ninety years ago:

> "At the short hole bunkers should abound. They should
> be so numerous and so fearful in aspect that the player
> delivers his tee shot almost without hope of escape."
> —John Low, *Concerning Golf*, 1903.

One visual trick of bunker design is to build up the lip of the greenside bunker higher than the level of the green to hide part of the surface from the approaching golfer. The 13th hole at Merion-East has a classic raised lip, making the green look more shallow than it is. These bunkers must be built with care, however; the reverse side of the contour should not be so abrupt that a ball just clearing the bunker is sent careening over the green.

Another favorite trick of mine to complicate bunker play is to leave some dead space between the bunker and the hole, either by locating the bunker slightly away from the green or by designing a fairly steep contour within the green. One bunker shot good players have mastered is the short explosion coming out high and stopping quickly; so a short bunker shot is actually easier for the low-handicapper than a pitch from the rough. It takes far more skill to play a long bunker shot to the proper tier of green, or to play a half-chip from the bunker that will run through the dead space and climb a slope near the pin. This bunkering strategy is particularly valuable for a three-shot hole: Bunkers slightly away from the green will penalize the off-line 2nd shot intended for the green, but shouldn't cause much hardship to the golfer playing the hole as a three-shotter.

ALTERNATE AND DOUBLE GREENS

Two unusual green configurations are the hole with alternate greens, and the double green serving two different holes. Both have been used in recent years by designers trying to draw attention to their courses.

The hole with alternate greens can be a solution where the designer wishes to create a very difficult pitch shot by building a small green, but is worried that such a green will not handle the anticipated volume of play—Pine Valley recently added an alternate green on its famous drive-and-pitch 8th hole for this reason. This is seldom recommended, however, because it is uneconomical. One 4,000-square-foot green would have as much area for pin placements as two 3,000-square-foot greens, because so much potential pin placement area is lost around the edge of the green. Yet the single green would cost only two-thirds as much to maintain. Thus alternate greens should be considered only where extremely difficult shot values are the rule of the course.

The double green has become even more common on modern courses; every modern example is compared by the publicists to the original double greens at St. Andrews. (Contrary to popular belief, they are extremely rare elsewhere in Scotland.) Public relations aside, there is no design logic for the double green. If two greens must be located in the same vicinity, they must be far enough apart to provide a safety margin from approach shots to the other hole, and it is much less expensive to maintain the safety buffer as a hazard than as part of an exceptionally large green.

THE PUTTING SURFACE

Putting is golf's great equalizer; indeed, it is so different from tee-to-green play that some of the most accomplished ball-strikers have wished that putting were banished altogether. Yet getting the ball in the hole is the very object of golf. Putting accounts for such a large part of the total score, both architect and superintendent have lavished great attention upon preparing the greens to perfection.

Just as the tee-to-green game would be dull without topography and hazards, the putting game would be lifeless if greens were compelled to be flat. But because the green is mowed so closely and the ball follows its every movement, the scale of undulations necessary to provide interest is much smaller than the scale of the other features on the course. A fairly modest slope (just one foot of rise in twenty linear feet) can create havoc on the green: The ball will not come to rest until it rolls to a flatter point, so the careful checking of levels is crucial to proper design.

The contours of a green cannot be properly designed without considering a related factor—the speed of the putting surface. For any given green speed, there is some degree of slope where there is insufficient friction to stop the ball from rolling downhill. For greens maintained at a fast pace by normal country-club standards, this threshold is about a 5-percent slope; that is the maximum slope you will find in the pin-placement areas of most greens designed by the master architects of yesteryear.

But when the green is cut short and the speed is at modern tournament standards—speeds which would have been impossible to achieve in 1930 without killing the grass—the same 5-percent slope that once made for a difficult downhill putt now carries the ball slowly but surely off the front of the green. At modern tournament speeds, any slope of more than 3 percent on the green is too steep for a pin placement, leaving little leeway for flowing designs and little margin for error in construction. Many modern architects are afraid to build heavily contoured greens because they do not have the ultimate say on the speed at which they are maintained.

I believe that the high green speeds coveted by many American club members are unnecessary, and sometimes counterproductive. On classic courses such as Augusta National, Winged Foot, and Pine Valley, the greens have steep slopes because the architects never intended them to be as fast as the members want them today. Furthermore, the shorter cut places the green under higher stress and makes it susceptible to more cultural problems.

Club members have become slaves to the readings of a Stimpmeter (a device used to measure green speed), and have lost sight of the fact that putting difficulty—the combination of slope and speed—and not green speed alone should set the standard for tournament play. Instead of removing the turf on hallowed greens and leveling them to cope with new green speeds, clubs would be better advised to raise their mowing heights a fraction and putt as the architects originally envisioned.

Just as the architect must worry about the maximum grade for putting, he must also worry about the minimum, and ensure that the surface of the green be designed to shed drainage water that might stagnate the soil. In the days before artificial irrigation, greens were often located in hollows because they held water to nurture the green, the origin of the classic "punch bowl." Today it is essential that the surface of the green be constructed without pockets retaining irrigation water, and that drainage around the green be directed away from its surface. The simplest way to accomplish this is to elevate the green slightly from its surroundings, but a cleverly chosen natural site may achieve the same objective.

Because subtle differences in grade have such great effect on the green, it is inevitable that the construction of a modern green must be a very artificial practice. The recommended method of construction, developed by the United States Golf Association's Green Section for turf research in the 1960s, involves the construction of three layers of imported soils to create a perched water table under the green, supplying the grass with sufficient moisture for sustained growth while releasing excess water and reducing the compactibility of the surface soil.

It must be said that the USGA method of construction was developed in a soil laboratory, and the theory of the perched water table is strained by the contoured surfaces common to putting greens. This is especially true given the difficulty of exactly replicating the contours for three separate layers of material, essential to the fluid mechanics of the system.

Most of the greens renowned for their excellent condition were built prior to the USGA's research, when conflicting theories of construction existed. Some fine greens even exist on unmodified ground, thanks to the natural existence of well-drained soil combined with good surface drainage to minimize problems. But one of the goals of putting-green maintenance is to produce consistent playing surfaces for all 18 holes, and for this to be achieved, construction along the lines of the USGA method is a worthwhile investment, especially as golf continues to grow in popularity.

To design the green's contours and plan the proper surface drainage are one in the same task. The ability to achieve this utilitarian goal while fitting the finished product into its surroundings, and rewarding good golf, is the hallmark of a great architect.

For both esthetic and practical reasons, the architect should avoid directing all of the drainage off the green at one point. Surface drainage must be directed away from the bunkers, since it would erode the sand from their faces, and a common mistake is to drain the entire green to the middle and then off the front, between guardian bunkers. The result is an approach constantly wet from irrigation water, inhibiting the bounced-in approach the opening suggests. It is advisable to break up the drainage into two or more watersheds, and to direct the runoff from each to a different spot.

Each watershed represents an area of the green where the hole may be located, and each may require a different approach shot depending on how it slopes in relation to the fairway. It is important for the architect to consider the utility of each area for pin placements before he has approved the green for seeding. In such pin-placement areas the green need not be level, as some writers have suggested. But the slope must not be too steep, as we have already discussed. In the name of equity, there should be plenty of places to locate the hole where the slope on the green does not change significantly, so that a three-foot putt will not change its break midway to the hole.

The minimum size of a usable pin placement is six feet in diameter. In practice, the area should be larger to allow the hole to be moved a bit to any side of the center while maintaining the three-foot buffer. By varying the size of the pin-placement areas, the architect will indirectly determine where the hole most often will be located.

Where a multilevel green with steep banks between levels is used, each level must be a bit larger than standard to allow for the ball to lose momentum when it is putted down from a higher level. Tom Simpson postulated that at least 75 percent of the green's surface should be flat enough to serve as a pin placement. While this rule may be broken on occasion, the

#16 St. Andrews—Old Course

#15 Royal Portrush—Dunluce Course.

Natural sand erosion at Tenby GC, Wales.

Dune Bunker, #6 St. Enodoc, England.

Sod-wall pot bunkers, #17 Muirfield.

"Fringed" look, Royal County Down, N. Ireland.

#10 Augusta National
(Mackenzie)

#13 Bel Air (Thomas)

#18 Pine Valley (Crump)

Heather is the primary component of the rough on many British courses, such as #15 Swinley Forest, England.

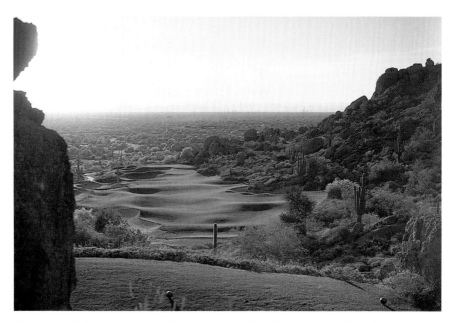

Because of the severity of desert terrain, bunkers are employed as a transition into the native desert at #1 Desert Highlands, Arizona.

Large specimen trees such as the elm behind #10 Winged Foot - East have great landscape effect.

Occasionally, trees can be used as a strategic hazard. At #2 Blairgowrie-Wee, two trees at the entrance to the green stymie the aerial approach. However, the hole will be without interest if the trees are lost.

A mound in front of the green deflects approaches to #4 St. Andrews-Old Course, but does not stymie recovery shots.

Water and artificial mounding force the golfer to play a high pitch at #7 PGA West - Stadium Course.

A narrow creek is just as effective a cross hazard as a large pond, without being as penal to the average golfer; its depth also permits attempts at recovery shots. (#4, Lancaster C.C., Pennsylvania, William Flynn, architect)

The green at #6 Crooked Stick is bulkheaded right to the edge of the hazard.

"The Pit", #13 North Berwick—West Links.

"The Dell", #6 Lahinch, Ireland.

architect should remember that the task of cutting the hole each day often falls to a 20-year-old green-crew member who knows little about golf, and whose favorite hobby is motorcycle racing.

Contours on the green are of two varieties: those that blend into larger external contours, and those entirely internal to the green. Contours blending into the surrounds may be somewhat bolder, since the edge of the green will be several feet away from any hole placement. All contours must be gentle enough to be mowed to the requisite height without scalping the grass. An occasional bold slope adds interest to putting, but it should be broad enough so as not to produce too many unpredictable bounces for the approach shot.

Despite all my discussion of pin placements, I think too much attention has been paid to their creation by some architects, whose greens suffer from the obvious appearance of artificiality. The best greens look like an unbroken series of rolls at first glance, and divide themselves into pin placements only under careful scrutiny. Sometimes the most difficult putt to read and hole is the one that appears nearly flat.

One of the biggest aids for blending the green into its surrounds, not often used by modern architects, is the roll off or flare at the edge of a green. On older greens they appear as natural extensions of the mounds and hollows in the green complex. They are more difficult to blend into the flatter pin-placement areas of modern greens, and they are much more difficult to construct using the three-layer USGA method. Nevertheless, such undulations add great interest to the short shots around the green, and provide incentive for placing the drive and shotmaking for golfers who know how to use flares to contain approach shots.

Many architects are capable of producing excellent plans, either by pen and ink or on the computer, but there is no substitute for a man in the field—the architect himself, the construction foreman, or the bulldozer operator—familiar with the character of good greens. Instead of making endless elevation checks to duplicate the letter of the plans, only to modify the result to please the eye, the fieldman can shape the ground like a sculptor until the green fits into the landscape, perhaps achieving a result the designer at a drafting board would never have visualized in all its subtleties. Not only the architect but his on-site representative should be familiar with the finest greens of championship courses, from St. Andrews to Pinehurst to Augusta. (A more complete list of greens worth study will be found in chapter 16.)

The student of design will observe that the most subtle and intricate greens are found on older golf courses. This is not so much a function of the equipment used in construction but rather the time factor. On early courses it took several days to shape each green with drag pans and teams of horses or mules, so the architect had time to mull over and adjust the subtleties of the green while it was being built. The same small-scale undulations can be created today with a small bulldozer or box scraper, but since a less detailed design can be built so much faster with a large bulldozer, many architects and construction companies expect the subtleties to take care of themselves, instead of working them out logically.

The best subtle contours can happen accidentally when hand-finishing a green, and these which separate the more characterful older courses from our modern products. Dr. Mackenzie used to tell the story of a contractor who built exceptionally natural-looking undulations, whose secret was that he "simply employed the biggest fool in the village and told him to make all the greens flat."

8

TEES

"The great thing about designing a golf hole is the architect gets to put the spectator or the player at a certain starting point. It is a perfectly controlled perspective, one of the few perfectly controlled perspectives in life. We put two tee markers down and we say, 'Stand here, golfer, and nowhere else, and you will look at what we put in front of you.'"

—STEVE WYNN, "The Story of Shadow Creek,"
USGA Green Section Record, March/April 1991.

The subject of tee placement would have been overlooked sixty years ago in a book of this kind. In golf's prehistoric days the ball was teed within two club lengths of the previous hole. In the early part of this century, the only real requirement was a relatively flat spot where a pinch of sand could be made to elevate the ball. On modern courses, great emphasis is placed on the proper design of teeing grounds.

The tee is the beginning point of every hole, and today's golf course operators place importance on it because the tee makes an immediate impression on the golfer. It is difficult to see why the turf conditions of a tee make much difference to the player; after all, the ball sits on a wooden peg. But we all know that playing from a bare surface or a rubber mat leaves us with a very poor impression. Thus the architect should strive to construct tees not only sufficient in size and substance for growing healthy turf, but in all respects pleasing to the eye.

A fault common to many otherwise outstanding courses is an insufficient teeing area to handle the volume of play. The same considerations regarding traffic apply to tees as they do to greens, but tees also suffer from the taking of divots, and from excessively shady conditions on parkland or wooded courses. Proper construction emphasizing drainage is paramount. While it is not common practice to build tees with imported soil as is done for the greens, soil conditions must be considered when determining the size of an adequate teeing ground.

The requisite size for tees is primarily a function of traffic. Each hole should have approximately one square foot of tee for every round of golf played during an average month of operation; this translates to between 3,000 and 5,000 square feet per hole on most courses. The suggested figure must be doubled on the par-3 holes, where divots are commonly taken. If multiple teeing grounds are used for each hole, 50 to 60 percent of the total should be provided on the middle tee (most commonly used by male golfers), 20 to 30 percent on the forward tee, and the remainder for the back tee.

The ideal surface grade of a tee is a subject of some debate. Modern tournament players have expressed their preference for the perfectly level tee on which their stance will promote neither a hook nor a slice. Such tees must be built with sub-drainage, at significant expense. The more common solution is to build a tee crowned or subtly pitched to one side to ensure proper surface drainage. The crowned tee has the additional advantage of allowing the clever player to tee his ball on a slope promoting a fade or a draw, depending on the shot pattern he favors. Another answer is to slope the tee in the same direction as the natural grade so as not to trap drainage from above on the tee. Some architects avoid building a tee which slopes from left to right and thus compounds the average player's tendency to slice. Care must be taken to ensure that players are not subtly induced to hit into trouble by tilting the tee in the same direction as a severe hazard.

The same consideration applies with equal force to constructing a rectangular tee aligned toward the rough instead of the middle of the fairway. It is not the architect's duty to help the player align himself, and it is perfectly alright to build a free-form tee facing no particular direction. But a narrow rectangular tee invariably causes players to align themselves parallel with its sides, and to deliberately align them toward trouble amounts to a dirty trick. Still, careless construction work results in such cheap psychological hazards on many courses.

Because the demand for well-conditioned teeing grounds is primarily grounded in esthetics, it is just as important esthetically that tees be designed in harmony with the surrounding land. Style has always been a matter of the architect's preference: Robert Trent Jones's courses were for years identified by extremely long, "runway" tees, while Lawrence Packard was among the first to experiment with free-form shapes, and George Fazio popularized the small, multiple teeing grounds currently in vogue. But the best designers subordinate their style to the landscape when necessary. Small tees look out of place and out of scale on a flat expansive area, just as long and narrow tees are impossible to reconcile with steep slopes.

Most architects build their tees well above the surrounding ground, often without good reason. A tee three or four feet in elevation may improve the visibility of the target area, but often the difference is negligible, or negated altogether if the forward tees are also elevated, blocking the view from further back. A grade change of six inches or a foot is all that is necessary to stop surface drainage from crossing the tee, and subtle slopes permit the banks of the tee to be easily maintained. The "gun-platform" tees found on modern courses are appropriate where tees are located in broken ground, such as on a desert course, but elsewhere they appear hopelessly out of place.

My personal preference is for large, free-form tees which can be designed in all sorts of intriguing shapes. Unlike long rectangular tees, a player at the back of the tee does not have to look across a field of divots in front of him. They also allow the superintendent to vary the angle of play slightly from day to day. The inclusion of sloped areas within the mown surface of the tee, by mowing down the banks at the sides of the tee or creating subtle tiers in the teeing area, can add visual interest to the foreground view of the player.

More important than the shape and size of tees is their placement on the course. Until now we have discussed the design of holes as if there were only one tee per hole, as the earliest courses provided. But in the modern game the range of abilities between the expert and the beginner is greater than ever. With only one tee per hole, most courses would be too easy to present a challenge to the expert, or too difficult for the average golfer to enjoy. Thus, alternate tees are provided on modern courses to appeal to both types of player.

The provision of forward tees also has an economic benefit to the club. For the sake of the beginner, every fairway must begin quite close to the tee so that a topped ball does not necessitate several swings from the rough. By shortening the course for the beginner, the architect reduces the length and acreage of fairway to be maintained. At the same time, the longer carries from the back tees make the course more interesting for the better players.

Architects have stopped making gender distinctions between teeing grounds, because such references aren't entirely fair. While the majority of women would be best served playing from the forward-most tees (as would some men), Nancy Lopez would certainly prefer a more challenging set of tees. In examining the plight of the average, 25-handicap woman golfer, architect Alice Dye shed light on the fact that we need an even greater variety of teeing grounds than exists today.

Mrs. Dye points out that the development of irrigated fairways has been hard on the shortest hitters, who relied on the roll of the ball for a significant portion of their total distance. Her research shows that the average (25-handicap) woman golfer hits the same club only about 80 percent as far as the average (17-handicap) man, yet the forward tees at most courses are set at about 80 percent of the *championship* tee length, rather than the middle-tee length. Under the present convention, the majority of par-4 holes measure between 300 and 360 yards from the forward-most tees—completely out of reach in two shots for the average woman, who hits her driver 150 yards. Whereas a modern Tour professional almost never hits a fairway wood shot, the average woman golfer is compelled to hit one as often as twenty times in each round. Just as the men have forward tees to bring the course within range of their strength, Mrs. Dye argues, there should be a set of tees between 4,800 and 5,200 yards in total length to bring holes within reach of the average woman golfer.

I agree that greater emphasis must be placed upon making courses playable and enjoyable for women, but I hesitate to endorse any recommended length as the cure-all. Modern designers have relied too much on forward tees to rectify real problems in the playability of their holes: forced-carry hazards, tight dogleg holes, or greens with no entrance and too small to hold a long approach shot. Whenever a golfer has no recourse but to play a lay-up shot to a specific point so he can get back into the flow of the hole, the hole needs modification. The architect's cry that the player "should have been playing from a forward tee" is a poor excuse.

Forward tees are not miracle makers, particularly when architects fail to account for the differences between golfers of similar overall ability. Just as Greg Norman and Lee Trevino rely on different strengths in their golf games, so do 15-handicap players, but the diversity of styles within this group is enormous. In the same Sunday foursome you are likely to find: a "gorilla" who can drive the ball 270 yards, but seldom straight; an elderly golfer who can't carry his tee shot more than 170 yards, but relies on a canny short game; and a golfer who can hit ten or twelve greens in regulation, but takes three to get out of every bunker and can't putt a lick. And all of those golfers will be playing their two-dollar Nassau from the same tees. Whether they play from the white, black, or fuschia tee markers, the architect has to make the course playable for all three. The architect cannot make all design decisions just to fit the mean player in the group.

In fact, the provision of multiple tees will force the thoughtful architect to be extra vigilant to ensure that players will be rewarded for a good drive from a forward tee. Too often the long hitter has to play an iron from the middle tee to avoid driving through the fairway and into trouble, taking away the one part of his game he needs to stay competitive.

In the final analysis, forward tees are meant to increase the average player's enjoyment of the game. There need be only sufficient teeing grounds for every class of player to have a chance to play all the shots of the game. The architect should recognize that human nature often will tempt golfers to play the course from further back than their games warrant. Back tees should be arranged so that the best golfer in the world will be tempted to make some exciting carries, and that the single-digit handicap player can also get around without losing his sanity or a dozen golf balls. The middle and forward tees should have a challenge and an interest of their own, or golfers will feel like they played a different and less interesting course. However, it is absurd and unnecessary to attempt to arrange the course so that every single player can get around in par figures, if only they were to play the right set of tees.

9

FAIRWAY
AND ROUGH

"Upon the manner in which the fairway is set—at any rate, at the longer holes—depends the greater part of the interest of the hole. If it appears plain and obvious, it is insipid and lacks character; but, laid out with ingenuity and imagination, it can please by the grace of its setting and intrigue the golfer by the particular problem that he has to solve to the best of his ability."
—H. N. WETHERED and TOM SIMPSON,
The Architectural Side of Golf, 1929.

The fairway does not, technically speaking, exist in the Rules of Golf. All the ground between tee and green, excepting hazards, is defined as "through the green"; the rules make no distinctions between fairway and rough. On the early links there was no clear line between the two, since sheep and rabbits do not establish a clear mowing pattern as they graze.

Long grass or "rough" is the most universal obstacle of golf courses, for the simple reason that no club wants to spend the money to mow and maintain the entire acreage of its course. Rough grass makes shots more difficult not only because it requires strength to swing the club through on line, but because the grass intervenes between ball and clubface, preventing the clean contact needed for backspin and control over the shot. The degree of difficulty of the rough depends on the type of grass and its height.

Rough of moderate height provides a suitable partial-stroke penalty for a drive out of the fairway. By making the subsequent shot more difficult to control, it reduces the player's chance of getting his approach close to the hole. However, the American obsession with making the punishment fit the crime has prompted clubs to maintain as many as three progressive heights of grass in the rough, so that the drive further off-line receives a greater penalty. For the beginning golfer this practice is like placing bunkers all down the side of the fairway, and all of the parallel mowing lines look unnatural.

Without some distinction between fairway and rough, every player would take the shortest route to the hole: the direct line. But if the fairway twists and turns, or is offset from the direct line, the situation becomes vastly more interesting.

Even where the fairway leads directly from tee to green, the margins need not be mowed in straight lines, as many clubs mistakenly do. Fairways cut in irregular-looking curves not only look more natural, but assist the player in locating a ball once in the rough. Extreme contour mowing has been employed by some architects to define target areas, reducing the maintenance costs for less used portions of the fairway. However, this method runs into trouble with alternate tees, and is unfair to golfers who hit the ball different lengths.

There are an infinite number of mowing patterns for every golf hole. Those proven to be most satisfactory follow the contours of the ground and the sweep of the eye. The natural tendency is for the edge of the fairway to follow the base of undulations, but it must be remembered that undulations will have more effect on the strategy of the hole if mowed short. A fairway with too many twists and turns looks unnatural; better plans follow a combination of basic themes.

The simplest variation on the straight hole is the offset

fairway, where most of the fairway is set to the right or left of the direct line. The direct line may be played if the player is willing to flirt with hazards. If the fairway is so offset that the direct line to the green is removed from its edge, then the hole can be classified as the well-known dogleg type. It is crucial in designing the dogleg for the architect to understand how far golfers can be expected to hit their drives, and to allow for sufficient variance between strong and weak players. This is especially true when thick trees or development land are contained within the crook of the dogleg. The short hitter must not be blocked from hitting a full second shot because of trees in the corner of the dogleg, nor must the strong player be forced to sacrifice his length from the tee because the fairway doglegs too quickly and trees block him from playing across the corner of the hole. Since tournament professionals now drive 250–300 yards, and high-handicappers anywhere from 150 yards on up, the dogleg hole is becoming harder to reconcile between the two.

The hole with a fairway set at an angle to the tee, such as the 11th at Oakland Hills-South, is especially interesting if the fairway is on relatively open ground, and there are no trees to force the golfer's drive down a particular line. On this hole a lateral ridge and a unique mowing pattern oblige the long hitter to make a sizeable carry to the fairway on the left of the ridge for the best angle to the green. If the player aims so he does not have to make the long carry, then a long drive will go through the fairway into the bunkers. Meanwhile, the short hitter can play safely to the right side of the fairway without making a long carry, but he is left with a long second shot from a very tough angle to hit and hold the green.

Finally, there is the delayed dogleg such as the famous 8th at Pebble Beach, where the fairway does not turn toward the green until well past the landing area for the tee shot. This arrangement of fairway forces the player who has not hit his best drive to either aim directly at the green with his second, and risk the penalty for falling short, or to minimize the carry

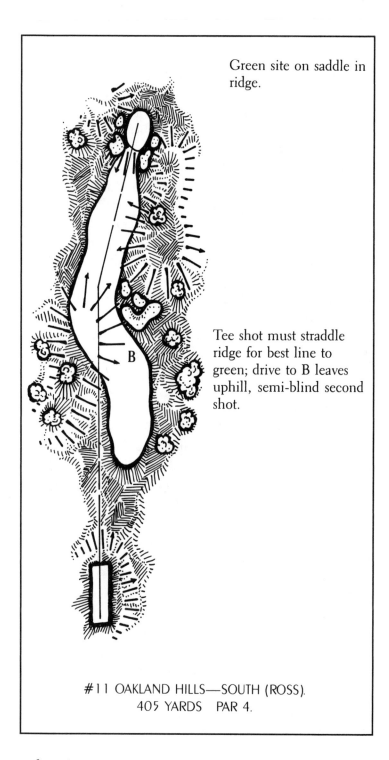

Green site on saddle in ridge.

Tee shot must straddle ridge for best line to green; drive to B leaves uphill, semi-blind second shot.

#11 OAKLAND HILLS—SOUTH (ROSS).
405 YARDS   PAR 4.

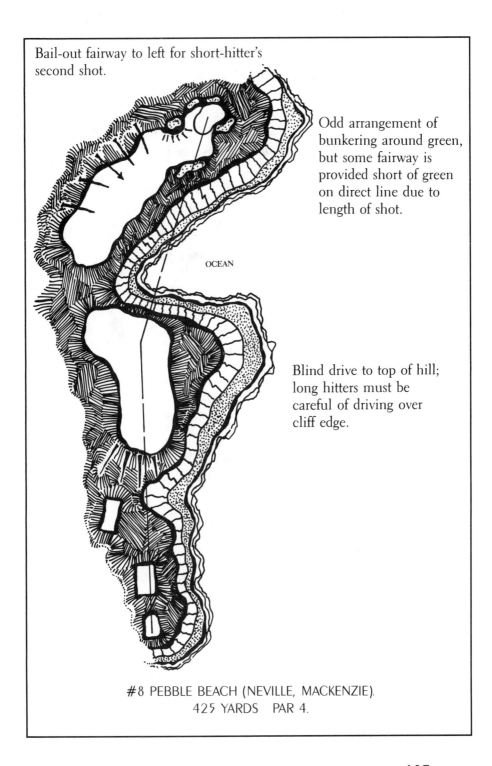

Bail-out fairway to left for short-hitter's second shot.

Odd arrangement of bunkering around green, but some fairway is provided short of green on direct line due to length of shot.

OCEAN

Blind drive to top of hill; long hitters must be careful of driving over cliff edge.

#8 PEBBLE BEACH (NEVILLE, MACKENZIE).
425 YARDS   PAR 4.

by playing along the fairway well to the left of the green and hoping to get a short third shot close to the hole.

A combination of the last two principles is illustrated by the wonderful 8th hole at Royal West Norfolk Golf Club in Brancaster, England. Bernard Darwin described it well in 1910:

> "I can think of no better simile to describe it than that of a man crossing a stream by somewhat imperfect stepping-stones, so that he has to make a perilous leap from one to the other. There are, as it were, three tongues or spits of land; on the first is the tee, on the third is the green, and between them lie strips of marsh, a sandy waste on which we may get a good lie, but are infinitely more likely to get a bad one. There is a safe, conservative method of playing the hole, which consists of a second shot along the second tongue, followed by a hop over the marsh on to the green. On the other hand, there is a more dashing policy, whereby we go out for a big shot off the tee, and try to reach the third tongue in our second stroke. . . . The wind, of course, has a great deal to say to our tactics, but, however we play the hole, we have got to hit all our shots as they should be hit, and that is as much as to say that the hole is a good one."
>
> —BERNARD DARWIN, *The Golf Courses of the British Isles*, 1910.

The most interesting aspect of this hole is that the middle-to-low handicap player may pull off a risky tee shot that just clears the marsh, only to be confronted with the choice of laying up with his second or attempting an even longer carry to reach the green. This may be one of the most magnificent of heroic holes in golf, but two forced carries make the hole quite severe for the average player. Were the hazard a pond, instead of a marshy area where the ball can usually be found and played back to dry land, the hole would be impossible.

Correctly proportional dimensions are just as important as the shape of fairway. This is a subject of much contention, since the consensus "ideal" width has become progressively

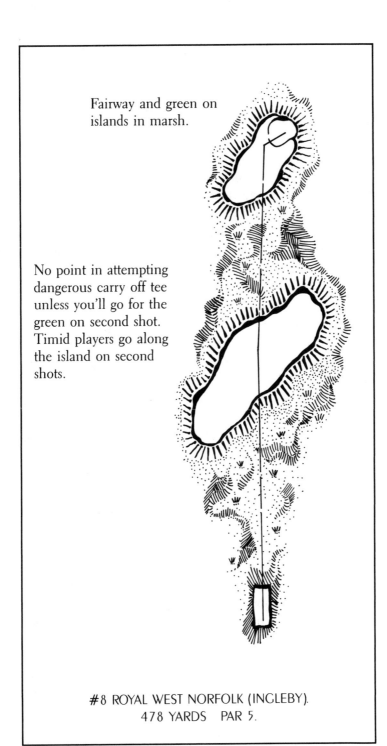

Fairway and green on
islands in marsh.

No point in attempting
dangerous carry off tee
unless you'll go for the
green on second shot.
Timid players go along
the island on second
shots.

#8 ROYAL WEST NORFOLK (INGLEBY).
478 YARDS   PAR 5.

129

narrower through the years. This trend is mostly a result of economic pressures. American clubs have set the standard for grooming fairways and it comes with a hefty per-acre price tag. Many clubs are forced to reduce the total acreage of fairways to keep their budgets within line. The two alternatives for reducing this acreage are to make the fairways narrower or to introduce islandlike target fairways. Unfortunately, neither is a satisfactory solution for the average golfer.

Just what constitutes a narrow fairway? George Thomas and other designers of his day advocated fairways 50 to 60 yards in width, but maintenance standards expected of fairway turf have increased over the years. As a result, acreage that can be affordably maintained has steadily grown smaller. The first step in this direction came with fairway irrigation systems. Fairways were narrowed to the limits that simple watering systems would cover—between thirty and forty yards across. The reduction in width was somewhat offset by the softer conditions, allowing an errant drive to stop rolling before it reached the rough. But today it is common at northeastern country clubs to see fairways only 25 to 30 yards wide—the same standard which the United States Golf Association sets for the U. S. Open Championship. Such a standard is hopeless for the beginning golfer, who drives the ball crooked so often he would be lucky to ever find the fairway on such a course.

Narrow fairways have also eliminated a strategic element. The most interesting strategic holes reward the player who can position his drive to a particular side of the fairway, giving himself the best angle to attack the length or slope of the green. Such holes are a primary reason that a course is considered worthy to host a championship. But in U. S. Open play today, the preparation of the course has undermined the design. The fairways are so narrow even the best players are not accurate enough to aim for a particular side, and the rough is so thick it is easier to hold the green from the wrong side of the fairway than from the rough on the correct side.

Everyone aims for the middle of the fairway, and a strategic element of the game is lost.

The alternative solution to reducing fairway acreage is to leave portions unmowed between the tee and landing area, or between landing area and green: the "target-golf" concept some modern architects advocate. Pine Valley is intended to serve as the ultimate model of "target golf," yet it is obvious to anyone who has played the course that this solution will never work for the average golfer. As soon as a player hits a poor tee shot and cannot make the leap to the next "island," the strategy of play deteriorates into a series of lay-up shots. Assuming that we have to allow for the weakest golfer, unable to consistently carry the ball more than 100 yards in the air, it is impossible to situate large gaps between target areas except between the fairway and the back tee. The concept of "target golf" is vastly more appealing than the reality, unless the area between the targets is playable by the average golfer.

It is possible for heroic holes to feature a "target golf" component, but an alternate route must be provided for the weak player. The all-time best example of such a hole was the par-5 4th at Charles Blair Macdonald's Lido Golf Club, now sadly no longer in its original form. The average golfer played the hole as a long three-shot affair around to the left, but the scratch golfer could attempt to reach the green in two via a small patch of fairway on the direct line, surrounded by impenetrable rough.

Holes like this would become monotonous for the average golfer if they were frequently encountered. Instead, subtle challenges provide the most interesting golf for the greatest number of golfers. The hole with a tilted green and a single, wide fairway might tempt the strong player to show off his strength when he ought to be playing for position, yet gives no undue hardship to the beginner taking the time to study it. This is the type of hole that should be our model for tomorrow.

The most important change to be made in American golf is not to reduce the acreage of fairways needing maintenance,

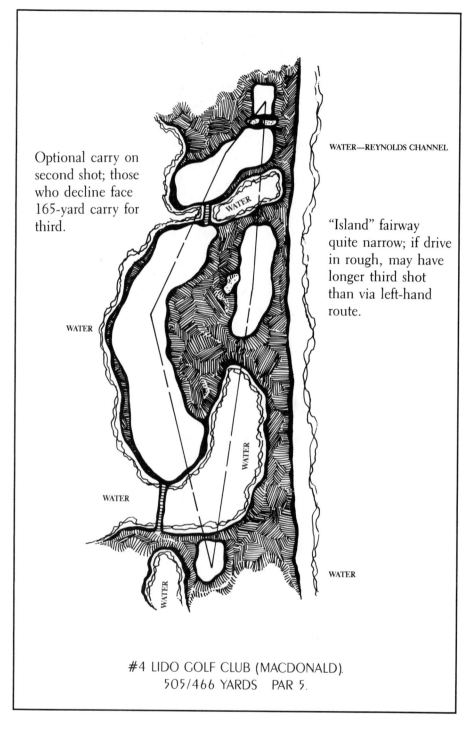

Optional carry on second shot; those who decline face 165-yard carry for third.

WATER—REYNOLDS CHANNEL

WATER

"Island" fairway quite narrow; if drive in rough, may have longer third shot than via left-hand route.

WATER

WATER

WATER

WATER

WATER

#4 LIDO GOLF CLUB (MACDONALD).
505/466 YARDS   PAR 5.

but to reduce the *standard* of maintenance expected on the fairway so the average golfer is provided with a reasonable target for his drive. Instead of concentrating maintenance efforts on the entire fairway, concentrate on maintaining the approach, and obtain courses both affordable and fair to the beginner.

10

BUNKERS
AND WATER HAZARDS

"Getting in a water hazard is like being in a plane crash—the result is final. Landing in a bunker is similar to an automobile accident—there is a chance of recovery."
—BOBBY JONES

Sand and water are traditional hazards in golf. The game evolved on the sandy links of Scotland, where bare patches of sand and narrow streams or burns were common features on the land. The preeminence of bunkers on artificial courses is a result of their ubiquity on the links (water seldom came into play on more than a couple of holes), the ease of their construction, and the relative penalty values that Bob Jones noted.

Today the golfer traveling to Muirfield or St. Andrews sees the remnants of natural bunkers in the form of "pot bunkers," many with faces of stacked sod. But in the early days bunkers were only eroded patches of sand, formed by animal scrapes

CONSTRUCTION DETAILS—SOD-WALL AND BULKHEADED BUNKERS.

The sod-wall bunker is built by stacking strips of sod, each set slightly back from the last to make a fairly steep but not vertical face, with the last strip of sod flush with the turf itself. The less-frequently-seen bulkheaded bunker is faced by railroad ties or boards set into the ground, again set slightly off the vertical to allow a recovery shot from under the face.

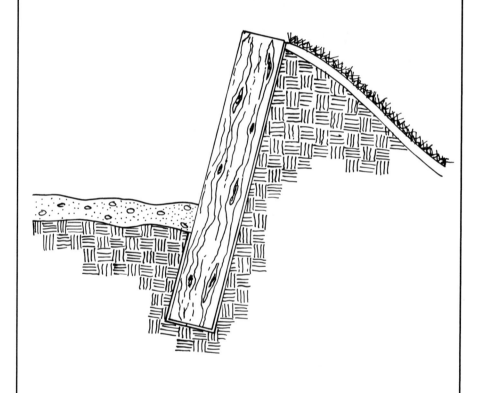

BULKHEADED BUNKER
(CROSS SECTION)

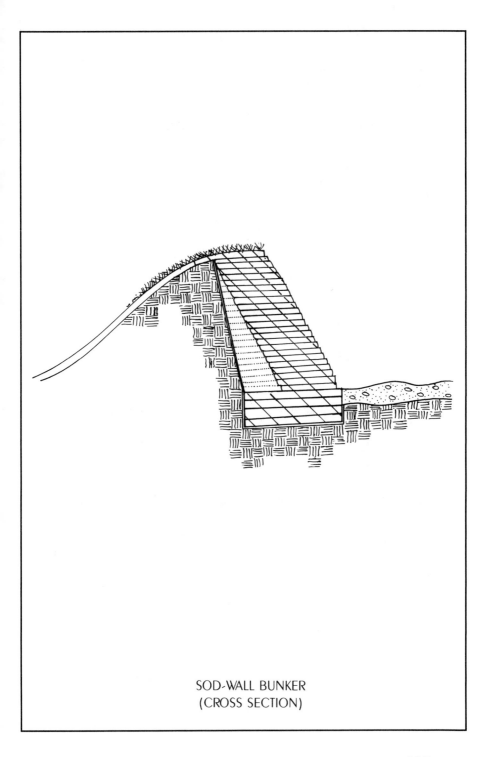

SOD-WALL BUNKER
(CROSS SECTION)

and enlarged by the wind. When courses were formalized and a bunker was agreed to add interest to the hole, it was stabilized by any available means, whether the sand flashed up naturally onto the slope of a dune, or had to be shored up by a grass face, stacked sod, or railroad ties.

It is no coincidence that the bunkers built by modern architects generally imitate one form or another of the bunkers found on the links.

BUNKERS—STYLE AND CHARACTER

"Bunkers, if they be good bunkers, and bunkers of strong character, refuse to be disregarded and insist on asserting themselves; they do not mind being avoided, but they decline to be ignored."

—JOHN LOW, *Concerning Golf*, 1903.

The style of bunkering currently in vogue among leading architects is the grass-faced bunker, where the sand lies flat at the foot of the slope. Publicists attribute these to an imitation of the "Scottish-style pot bunker," though in fact the first bunkers on the links were sand-faced scrapes eroded from the tops of dunes. Architects defend the style on the grounds that it eliminates the labor-intensive job of raking sand back up onto the face of the bunker, even though mowing the steep grass faces of bunkers (especially if they are covered with fast-growing bluegrass or Bermuda) is often as labor-intensive and more dangerous.[1]

The most common reason for the prevalence of grass-faced bunkers is that they require less design supervision than flashed-sand bunkers, where white sand creates a three-dimensional

---

[1]There are many former golf course maintenance workers walking around today missing one or more toes, the result of an accident with a fly mower on a steep bunker face.

shape that demands careful consideration. Many modern architects, with their busy schedules, don't want to spend time on such details. This is in strong contrast to the age of Mackenzie, Tillinghast, George Thomas, Dick Wilson, and Robert Trent Jones, whose work was instantly identifiable by their distinctive styling of bunkers.

Too many designers stick to their own trademark bunkers, without much thought to what style would best suit a given property. Grass-faced or sod-wall bunkers work well on open sites, such as the links, where their shadows give definition and where an intricate pattern of sand and grass would be lost against the vastness of the sky. Yet there is no question that artistically shaped sand-faced bunkers contrast beautifully with the dark backgrounds of a wooded golf course setting. The character of the soil also plays a part in the final analysis: pot bunkers may be dug in well-drained soils, but on heavy land the floor of the bunker must be carefully drained by raising it above the surrounding grade.

In the old days, an architect's bunkering style usually hinged on the issue of distance perception. Bunkers with flashed-sand faces stand out in the landscape, and give the golfer a sense of distance when set beside a green. On the other hand, depth perception on the links is very difficult because the lack of background features and the folds in the ground obscure the bunkers from view. Thus Tom Simpson and Charles Blair Macdonald, who spoke of deceiving the golfer's perception of distance, used bunkering styles showing little sand; while George Thomas and Alister Mackenzie, whose philosophy was to enhance the golfer's perception, were noted for their bold sand-faced hazards. Today, when golfers have yardage books to guide them, the point is largely moot.

Yet the character of the bunkering still has a significant effect on the difficulty of recovery shots, and therefore on the course's strategic value. Bunkers with a bottom of flat sand present difficult recoveries only when the face is terribly steep or the depth is exceptional. A full variety of difficult bunker shots includes downhill lies in the sand, buried or "fried-egg" lies, and occasional odd stances. These are part of the game only when the interior of the bunker is contoured, as in the flashed-sand variety. Without an occasional misfortune, good players are so proficient at recovering from bunkers they have lost value as a hazard; you may even overhear Tour players exhorting an errant shot to "get in a bunker!" because it presents an easier recovery than an uneven lie in the rough.

Bunkers are more strategically interesting than hazards like water and out-of-bounds because the penalty varies with the recovery skills of the golfer. The good player can be aggressive in attacking the hole near a bunker when he is confident of getting up and down from the bunker even if he should find it. For golfers who have no confidence in the sand, a deep bunker can extract an even greater penalty than water, because the player must get himself out of the hazard. Once the fundamentals are mastered, the ability to recover from the sand is perhaps the most important skill separating low and high handicappers; it is impossible to play a good shot while worrying about the consequences of a bad one into a bunker. It is hard to believe how little time average golfers spend improving their sand play, or how little attention is devoted by clubs to maintaining a good practice bunker.

The other profound influence on bunker play has been the change in attitude toward maintenance. Modern superintendents bend over backwards to maintain bunkers in flawless condition, and architects specify sand of consistent quality to minimize bad lies. Twenty years ago this was hardly a consideration. Architects were of a less conciliatory frame of mind,[2] and some fine courses, such as Southern Hills, were notorious for their bad sand.

---

[2]Henry Fownes, creator of Oakmont, designed a special bunker rake to prepare the sand in furrows and guarantee difficult lies, while Charles Blair Macdonald once suggested that "a herd of elephants" be trampled through the bunkers before a championship was to be played.

Improving the quality of bunker sand has had an additional psychological benefit: Because players aren't worried about what kind of lie they might get in a bunker, they can stand over their approach shots with confidence and aim for the flag without fear. This was once the province of only the greatest scramblers in the game, a strategy Gary Player or Tom Watson could adopt, but for most good players was reckless.

I am sure one of the reasons Pine Valley is acclaimed as the greatest of today's courses is that the bunkers are infrequently raked, making it one of the only courses where hazards really are hazards. Still, I can't imagine club members happily agreeing to the elimination of bunker rakes, any more than I can imagine the Tour forbidding players from charting yardages, forcing them to use their own judgment in club selection as Bob Jones and Ben Hogan did.

BUNKER PLACEMENT

"It is much too large a subject to go into the question of the placing of hazards, but I would like to emphasize a fundamental principle. It is that no hazard is unfair wherever it is placed.

A hazard placed in the exact position where a player would naturally go is frequently the most interesting situation, as then a special effort is needed to get over or avoid it."

—Alister Mackenzie, *Golf Architecture*, 1920.

In the early days of golf, the position of bunkers was a given and holes were designed around them. In modern construction, the architect chooses where to place his bunkers to accent the lay of the land. Indeed, bunkers are the one form of hazard easily introduced into the landscape wherever the architect feels they add to the interest of the hole.

Bunkers are conceived for a variety of purposes. They can

be built to penalize a particular missed shot, or to keep players from getting into worse trouble, such as when a bunker at the edge of a ravine prevents a marginal shot from becoming lost. They can also be built for visual purposes: to assist the player in lining up a semi-blind shot, or to scare the golfer away from a dangerous area where two holes converge.

Bunkers built primarily for visual purposes can be misleading or awkward in appearance. Large target bunkers built into mounds at the outside of a dogleg are commonly used by modern architects to "turn" the hole; but if such an impressive hazard had existed on the property, surely the hole would be designed so players would have to contend with it. The most impressive hazards on British links—Hell bunker at St. Andrews, the Cardinal at Prestwick, or the original Maiden at Sandwich or Soup Bowl at Rye—are located right in the middle of a hole, where the player must either carry them or go well around.

This is the principal value of the bunker: to influence the golfer's choice of a line of play, and to dole out punishment if he fails to heed the hazard. However, it is important to qualify this statement with the fact that different players hit the ball different distances. Since it is impossible to place a bunker to affect all the players all the time, we must only worry about affecting some of the players some of the time. Any bunker along the general line of play can be defended as an added interest, as long as they do not appear at the same distance from the tee so often as to be unfair to golfers of a certain strength.

The cornerstone of the modern strategic school of design is that average golfers make their own trouble, and that fairway bunkers 100 to 200 yards off the tee serve to make the game more frustrating for them. Yet courses designed strictly along these lines are often rather boring for the average golfer. Every player should experience the thrill of the game, as John Low described it:

"The greedy golfer will go too near and be sucked in to his destruction. The straight player will go just as near as he deems safe, just as close as he dare. . . . The fine player should be just slipping past the bunkers, gaining every yard he can, conquering by the confidence of his own 'far and sure' play. The less skilful player should wreck himself either by attempting risks which are beyond his skill, or by being compelled to lose ground through giving the bunkers a wide berth."
—JOHN LOW, *Concerning Golf*, 1903.

This is the appeal of the Old Course at St. Andrews. Wethered and Simpson captured the essence of the course:

"St. Andrews is difficult, not because bunkers are placed to catch inaccurate shots, but because the result of a misadventure is to make the next shot infinitely more difficult than it otherwise would have been. . . . To choose a line of play is, as often as not, very much a choice of evils. Each successive shot must be played on its own merits."
—WETHERED and SIMPSON,
The Architectural Side of Golf, 1929.

The only thing keeping St. Andrews from being the perfect strategic course is that the visibility of the pot bunkers is quite poor. This does not affect the member of the Royal & Ancient Golf Club, who has a clear mental picture of each hole. But the unfamiliar visitor must rely on the advice of his caddie, and in so doing is denied the interest of making his own tactical decisions—the very feature that makes the course so outstanding for those who have come to know their way around it.

Visibility is only one of several ways in which outstanding bunkering relates to topography. While the placement of bunkers is usually discussed in terms of proper distances, the architect should be more concerned with how the lay of the land will influence play, and designing bunkers to complicate the situation. Often the most satisfying holes are those where the bunkers are set into natural slopes facing the line of play, and the tee is placed and the green shaped to fit a strategy revolving around the bunkers.

The most natural-looking bunkers are set into the crest of a rise or a facing slope, wherever it falls on the hole, to look as if they are the product of wind erosion. On flatter ground, it is easy enough to construct a slight mound into which the bunker is set. But it is usually futile to attempt the same thing on a severe downgrade, particularly where it is out of sight from the tee, in order to locate the bunker at what the architect decides is an ideal distance from the tee. In such a case, it is better to set the bunker into the crest, even if it's only 170 yards from the tee. Let that be one of the driving holes of particular interest to the shorter hitter, and set up the second shot to interest the long driver.

An alternative is the bunker set into the face of a hollow or a valley running across the fairway, where the contours of the ground draw the short running ball in toward the bunker, as might a whirlpool. The pot bunkers at Muirfield and St. Andrews are notorious for this gravitational influence. If cleverly placed, such bunkers can exert their influence over a large portion of the fairway, even though the hazard itself is small enough to be overlooked by a golfer on the tee. However, it is of utmost importance that such bunkers are placed in the face of a slope where drainage water from the fairway will run around them, instead of located in the bottom of the hollow where they will be flooded.

At the turn of the century, one school of design thought that a course should be built without bunkers at first, only to be added after the committee studied how golfers attacked the unadorned hole. Sometimes they had the wrong idea, witness Herbert Leeds at Myopia Hunt Club:

> "When the drive of a long hitter was sliced or hooked
> Leeds would place a marker on the spot and a new trap

filled with soft white Ipswich sand would appear. This resulted in some holes being praised by British professionals as the most skilfully trapped in the United States."

—Letter, Edward Weeks to Geoffrey Cornish,
August 2, 1979, as published in *The Golf Course.*

Though most bunkers of such origin would have been placed too far from the tee to disturb the average golfer's drive, Leeds's hazards were penal rather than strategic in concept. But other noteworthy courses were built where the bunkers were added several years after construction, Kingston Heath in Australia, bunkered by Mackenzie, being perhaps the most notable. Some of the most compelling bunkers at St. Andrews were additions by evolution. Where a particular hollow in the fairway tended to collect drives and many divot scrapes were taken, it eventually became impossible to grow grass and the area was formalized into a bunker.

Unfortunately, this method of design is impractical because of the economic advantages of simultaneously constructing the green complex and hazards, and considering drainage as part of the design problem. The best golf architect works out the entire problem in his head beforehand.[3]

As an example of working with the lay of the land, say that a given hole is routed along a moderate right-to-left sideslope, where all shots will tend to run to the left after landing. The architect immediately realizes that the two common shot patterns, hook and fade, will produce two different results; the hook will continue to run down the slope, gaining extra distance, while the fade will strike the hill and quickly stop, offering more control.

The simplest strategic hole for such a situation would have the green tilted the same as the fairway; this would favor an

---

[3]Many architects, however, need to spend more time watching golfers play their courses, to ensure that the line of play they visualized is the same one which the golfers identify.

Green A favors approach
into slope from left.

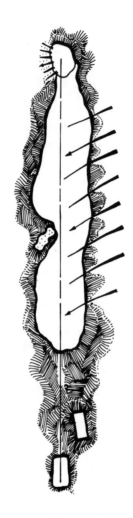

GENERIC HOLE A.

Tilt of the green favors an approach from
left of fairway, so the primary fairway hazard is
placed at left. Forward tees are set to the
right to hit around bunker.

Green B has entrance on right, so best drive is also to right.

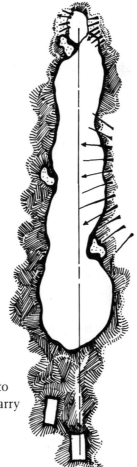

Forward tees placed to minimize need for carry over fairway bunker.

GENERIC HOLE B.

Bunker defends front left of green, so the best approach is from right-center of fairway; therefore a bunker guards the right side of the landing area. Note that forward tees are placed to the left on this hole to minimize carry over the fairway bunker.

approach from the left side of the fairway, hitting uphill into the slope of the green. The strategic fairway bunker would be placed along the left of the fairway. This bunker might be placed along the edge of the fairway at the limit of a good drive, to force the better player to choose between laying up or risking the bunker to gain a shorter approach. Or it may stick out into the fairway just short of a good drive, so the strong player could try to carry the fairway bunker, and the accurate player could try to use the slope of the fairway to curve a drive around it.

Another approach is when the architect decides to build up the left side of his green and place a large bunker at the foot of the slope to favor the player who could fade his drive to the right side of the fairway so he wouldn't have to carry the greenside bunker with his second shot. No fairway bunker would be necessary to this strategy, as the slope of the fairway and the presence of the greenside bunker make clear the best line of play. The architect might complicate matters by adding a carry hazard along the right side of the fairway, or even by adding a fairway bunker on the left to make things more difficult for the player who trusts his ability to carry his approach shot over the greenside hazard.

An architect may choose to place fairway bunkers by looking at the problem backward from the green, a strategy particularly useful for long holes. For example, on a 550-yard par-5, if it fit into the landscape I might place the only fairway bunker 300 yards from the back tee—out of range for nearly everyone except the long hitter, who would have to avoid it if he is going to get to the green in two shots. Then the short hitter would not be handicapped by having to play three shots which must avoid bunkers, when the long hitter has to play only two.

Similarly, a bunker 40 to 50 yards short of the green on a long hole, either a long par-4 or a par-5, can add visual interest and strategy to the approach. Such a hazard is especially valuable to penalize the golfer who flails away for the green,

Bunkers at right of green make difficult third shot for player who attempts to skirt fairway hazard and slices.

Cluster of bunkers short of green forces short driver to choose between laying up or trying to skirt past right edge.

Short driver needs to aim over bunker in corner of hill for clear path to green.

#5 YARRA YARRA (MACKENZIE).
437 YARDS   PAR 4.

149

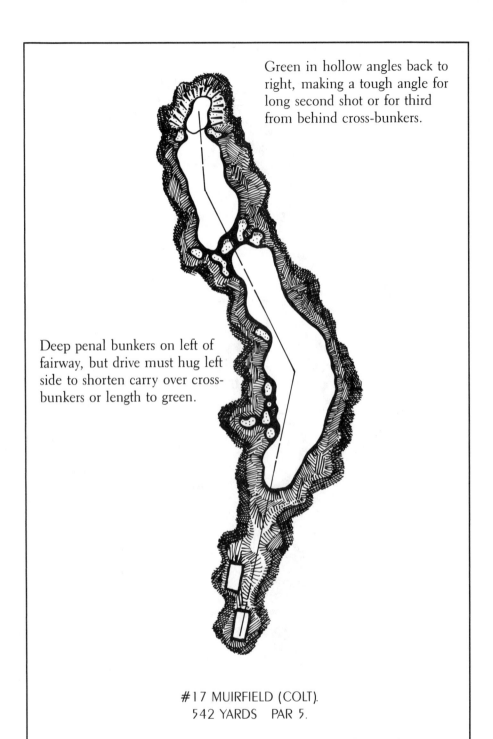

Green in hollow angles back to right, making a tough angle for long second shot or for third from behind cross-bunkers.

Deep penal bunkers on left of fairway, but drive must hug left side to shorten carry over cross-bunkers or length to green.

#17 MUIRFIELD (COLT).
542 YARDS   PAR 5.

and falls drastically short, with one of the toughest shots for good players: the long bunker shot.

The best bunkers intrude right up to, or actually cross, the ideal line to the hole, forcing the golfer to play wide and add distance to the hole if he does not want to risk them. Perhaps no better example exists than the par-5 17th at Muirfield; a cluster of deep pot bunkers forces the safe drive out to the right, where the long hitter will be out of reach of the green, and where the average golfer will even have difficulty carrying the cross-bunkers with the second shot.

It is curious that very few American courses feature such critically placed fairway hazards; Riviera and The National are the only two which come to mind. This is because the fairway has become a sacrosanct part of the American course. Overseas, there is still much of the spirit of early golf, when all the ground "through the green" was roughly of equal value. Consequently, on American courses it is rare to see a bunker across the fairway or within the fairway, even though such hazards are to be found all over the links.

The bunker in the middle of the fairway is an especially controversial topic. It should certainly not be overused, but it is the ideal solution for a wide and flat landing area where a regular-width fairway with flanking bunkers would not fill the space. A single fairway bunker placed right where the golfer would most like to drive (or just off-center), with plenty of fairway around it to all sides, increases the interest of the hole tenfold. The par-4 16th hole at St. Andrews, defended by a cluster of fairway bunkers known as the Principal's Nose, is the classic example of this arrangement. The weakest players do not worry because they will not reach the central hazard with their drives; others will aim straight at it, confident that their usual inaccuracy will prevent them from harm. For the accomplished golfer, the key to the hole is the green, oriented so that the approach is much easier from the right, where the hole is bordered by out-of-bounds. Some of the better players play short of the bunker for safety, and are content to play a

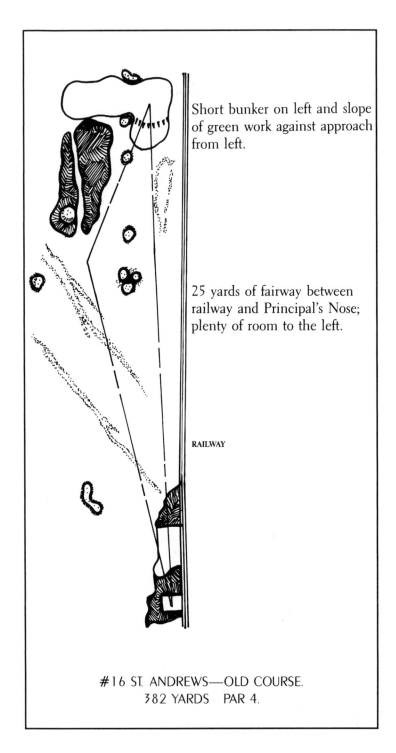

Short bunker on left and slope of green work against approach from left.

25 yards of fairway between railway and Principal's Nose; plenty of room to the left.

RAILWAY

#16 ST. ANDREWS—OLD COURSE.
382 YARDS   PAR 4.

152

longer club for their approach shot. Others may try to use their power to drive over the hazard, while some will call on their accuracy to slip by the bunker. In other words, every player has the chance to avoid the hazard in his own way.

Still, the central-fairway bunker is usually greeted with scorn by low-handicap golfers, who believe that the sole purpose of golf architecture is building a course that separates good shots from bad ones. In this narrow perspective, a bunker right in the middle of their landing area is simply not kosher, though they would not object to a bunker in the same location if the fairway were doglegged around one side of it. It is the extra option that confuses them, the fact that a shot to either side will escape retribution. To some this "weakness" gives too much scope for luck, but there cannot be a bunker to punish every missed shot—hundreds would be needed. Mackenzie compared the bunkers on a golf course to the fielders in cricket: "In both games it is only a proportion of bad shots that get punished, but notwithstanding this the man who is playing the best game almost invariably comes out on top."[4]

The mechanics of golf shots also influence the placement of bunkers. If four bunkers of equal size were placed at the sides of a diamond-shaped green, each would catch a different proportion of shots. The right front bunker would catch the weakly sliced ball, accounting for probably 40–50 percent of the average golfer's misses. The left rear bunker might catch another 25–30 percent of shots missing the green, the result of a pulled iron shot which tends to finish long as well as left. The front left bunker would catch the fat or underclubbed pulled shot, slightly less common than the strong pull. Least active of all would be the back right bunker, since the shot would have to be significantly overclubbed for the faded approach to reach it.

[4]Perhaps the difference between American and British attitudes can be drawn along the lines of our national games. Cricket is a far more forgiving game for the offensive player than baseball, where "outs" are more frequent than hits.

Many architects appreciate the role of shot mechanics and choose to place the majority of their bunkers on the left of the course, smoothing the path for less accomplished golfers. One reason to avoid this convention is that accomplished golfers have developed a shot pattern of their own. The broad decision to omit hazards at the front right of the green, with the goal of making things easier for the average golfer, might unduly favor the player who fades the ball over the golfer who plays a draw. Thus the theory that the majority of hazards should be placed to the left of the course is best avoided. The Old Course at St. Andrews, the most interesting course I have seen for both beginner and expert, has the great majority of its fairway hazards on the right, with greenside hazards on the left to ensure that the player hooking his tee shot into the safety of the double fairways has to carry a hazard with his second shot to get at the hole.

In bunker placement as in every other aspect of golf architecture, variety is the key. When bunkers are placed according to a pattern, the course is unsound and artificial in appearance. If they are placed in harmony with the topography, they add interest through their diversity, and complete the strategic puzzle.

WATER HAZARDS

Water hazards can provide the most dramatic moments in golf, or the most frustrating. Where beautiful natural water hazards exist on a property, it would be a shame not to use them to add interest to the golf holes. Yet such is the case on many modern courses. On the one hand, the developer wants to reserve lake or ocean frontage for other uses, and confine the golf course to interior property; on the other, environmental groups argue that the lake or stream must be protected from potential golf course runoff.

On some projects it is necessary to create ponds and other water-retention areas where none naturally exist to provide for course drainage, or to supply water for the irrigation system. If the creation of a water hazard is not necessary for either of these purposes, the architect must consider whether the expense is worthwhile—especially since too much water on the brain makes things so much more difficult for the weaker player.

Many developers and public-course operators insist on a certain amount of water because the public equates water hazards with "better" courses. But pandering to the public's expectations makes our courses conventional rather than outstanding.

The history of water hazards can be traced to the narrow streams or burns found running across the links on their way to the sea. Most Scottish links are similar to St. Andrews in this regard, with water coming into play on just a couple of the holes. It must be remembered that the featherie ball floated, and it was possible to play from the hazard in the "hit as you find it" spirit of British golf.

The small pond near the 5th green on the Old Course at Sunningdale, England, was the first artificially constructed water hazard, built by Willie Park in 1900. Through the so-called golden age of golf architecture, water hazards were found infrequently on great courses other than those which ran along the shore. In fact, several of the world's great courses, including Royal Melbourne, Muirfield, and Olympic (Lake), have no water hazards whatsoever.

The first architect to use water hazards to any great extent was Robert Trent Jones in the late 1940s, who saw them as the perfect hazard for his heroic school of golf design. Jones also saw the penal value of water as a way to recapture some of the stroke value which had been lost to thirty years of improvements in golfing equipment, most notably the acceptance of steel-shafted clubs and the invention of the sand wedge. He has described water as his "favorite hazard," and it is an important feature on both his original courses (Mauna Kea, The Dunes) and his redesign work (Oakland Hills, Augusta National). Some critics believe Trent Jones used too much water in his designs. The Bobby Jones quote which begins this chapter was something of an admonishment directed at Trent Jones while they were collaborating on the design of Peachtree Golf Club in Atlanta.

In the modern era of design, the use of water hazards has gone out of control. In part due to the golf course boom in Florida, where water hazards had to be created to drain the golf course and the surrounding development, the water hazard became a fashion slavishly accepted by golf architects, they even built 50-foot dams on hillsides to create a water hazard if none existed naturally. Florida ultimately gave us the island 17th hole on the TPC at Sawgrass (not a bad hole for the 71st of a major championship, for which it was designed, but in every other respect the germ starting the plague of island greens), and Old Marsh Golf Club, where water comes into play on 27 of the regulation 36 shots through the green. When water is overused to this extent, the litany of lost balls and lateral drops becomes tiresome and the marsh gets very old, indeed.

Water is not an ideal golfing hazard. It creates an unplayable situation, when the very nature of the game is to play the ball from wherever you have hit it, and when recovery shots are one of the most exciting in the game. Water hazards should therefore be used sparingly, and only under the strictest of design controls.

Three factors must be considered when designing holes around a water hazard. The hazard must be visible—the worst thing in golf is to incur a penalty stroke when the danger was not obvious. There must always be a way around the hazard, because for beginning players the forced carry may amount to an impossible barrier. And the effect of the hazard should be maximized for the scratch player, who is so adept at recovering from bunkers that only the water hazard can instill the fear of costing him a full stroke.

Visibility is an obvious issue when water hazards are involved, but it is often overlooked. The danger exists not only when there is a rise in the fairway before the green, but also on flat ground when the hazard is small. For this reason, small ponds dug for drainage near a green or the landing area of a fairway are seldom used by modern architects.

A forced carry over water is also best avoided, though modern regulations prohibiting the filling of wetlands may offer no alternative. If an area of marsh or open water must be hurdled by a golf hole, it is best to arrange this on the tee shot; a forward tee can be located at the brink of the hazard to minimize the carry, and another can be placed across the hazard to serve the weakest players. When the forced carry must be made on the approach to the green, the golfer having hit a poor drive must often lay up with his second in fear of not making the carry; and if the carry is more than 75 yards, it is possible that the beginning golfer will not be able to make it if the lay-up shot is not played right to the edge of the hazard, a very difficult shot to judge.

Ideal water holes tempt the golfer to flirt with the hazard in order to gain a significant advantage for the next shot—in other words, holes of heroic design. In most cases this involves an optional carry. On the famous 16th hole at Cypress Point, California, the golfer must choose between attempting to reach the green with a long carry over the ocean's edge, or playing an iron safely to the right and being content with a four. On the par-5 16th on Pete Dye's River course at Blackwolf Run, Wisconsin, the three-shot route to the green gives the river a wide berth, but an ideally located tree forces the long hitter to carry a slight bend in the river if he is to get home in two.

One problem with the diagonal water hazard is that the scratch player is generally too smart to fall victim to it: he plans

Green is large enough to receive a 220-yard shot, but three-putting is also common.

Fairway to left for short hitters, but a pulled shot which could have reached green will go over cliff on left.

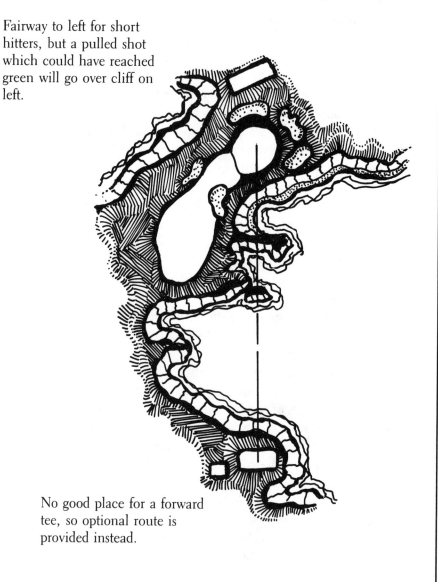

No good place for a forward tee, so optional route is provided instead.

#16 CYPRESS POINT (MACKENZIE).
219 YARDS   PAR 3.

Green bulkheaded high above river, creating elevation for deep bunker at right.

RIVER

Tree on left stymies "middle of the road" second shot, forcing player to choose between going for green to left of tree, hitting full second shot past tree on right for half-wedge approach, or laying back so tree can be carried on pitch.

TREES

Steep slope had to be terraced to provide best alignment of fairway.

Long waste bunker on left penalizes a draw which turns into a hook; height of bulkhead means golfer will be left with a long third, unless he dares to play a fade down the line of the bunker with a long iron.

#16 BLACKWOLF RUN—RIVER COURSE (DYE).
560 YARDS   PAR 5.

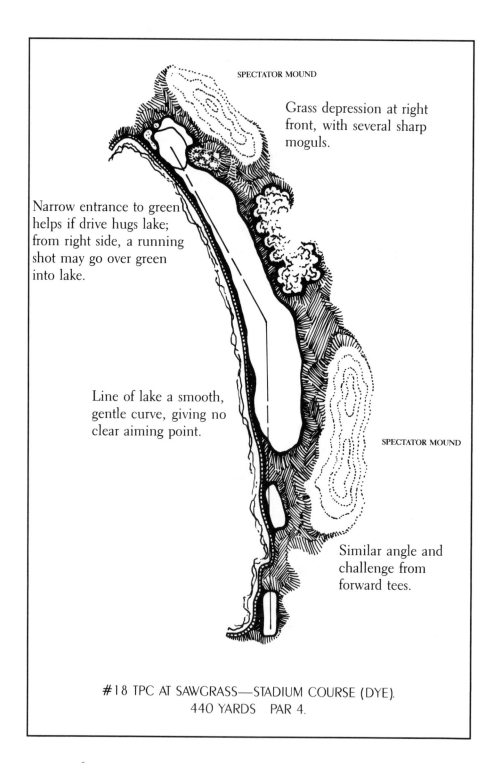

SPECTATOR MOUND

Grass depression at right
front, with several sharp
moguls.

Narrow entrance to green
helps if drive hugs lake;
from right side, a running
shot may go over green
into lake.

Line of lake a smooth,
gentle curve, giving no
clear aiming point.

SPECTATOR MOUND

Similar angle and
challenge from
forward tees.

#18 TPC AT SAWGRASS—STADIUM COURSE (DYE).
440 YARDS   PAR 4.

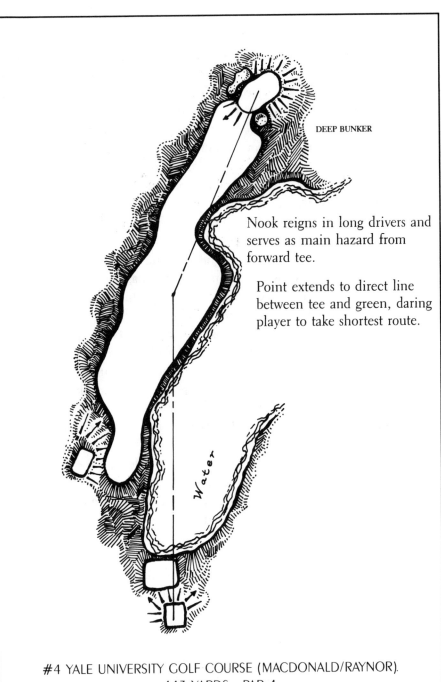

DEEP BUNKER

Nook reigns in long drivers and serves as main hazard from forward tee.

Point extends to direct line between tee and green, daring player to take shortest route.

Water

#4 YALE UNIVERSITY GOLF COURSE (MACDONALD/RAYNOR).
443 YARDS   PAR 4.

his attack so that a well-struck drive will clear the hazard even if it is somewhat off-line.[5] Professionals have the most trouble with hazards that describe a gentle arc, so that a ball pushed or pulled just slightly from the ideal line will wind up in the hazard, as on the tee shot of the 18th of the TPC at Sawgrass. Another possible solution is found on the 4th hole at Yale, where the hazard cuts back into the line of play to narrow the driving area for the exceptionally long hitter.

On some holes, water narrows the fairway to demand careful placement of the tee shot. The 10th at Donald Ross's Highlands Country Club is an excellent case in point. A slashing stream cuts in right at the corner of the dogleg, giving the golfer a choice between driving into the narrowed area, or laying up with an iron off the tee and leaving himself a fairway wood to get home in regulation.

Robert Trent Jones's famous 13th hole at The Dunes in Myrtle Beach, South Carolina, combines both principles outlined above. The hole describes a boomerang around the perimeter of Singleton Lake. It is impossible to carry the lake from the tee, but by placing a tee shot close to the edge of the pond on the right it is much easier to make the carry on the second shot. The golfer who plays safely to the left off the tee must often play safely again with his second, leaving the green out of range with his third shot. Holes like this will be rare indeed in the future, because the strategic filling along the shoreline of the lake which produced this ideal design is strictly forbidden today.

One modern trend associated with water hazards is the use of stone or railroad-tie retaining walls to define the edge between land and water. These bulkheads have been widely

---

[5]In this regard, the architect who places bunkers on the opposite side of a fairway requiring a diagonal water carry is defeating his own design. The better player will aim either to the right or left of the bunker, but he will seldom go in it. In the meantime, the bunkers give him a visual reference point to reassure his judgment of the water carry.

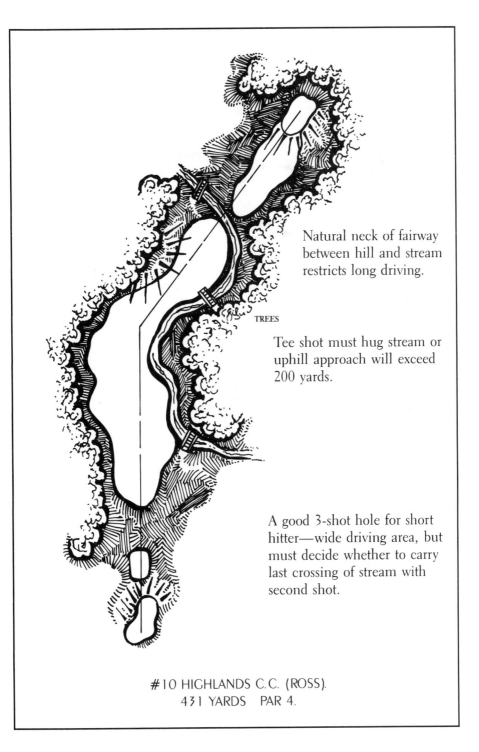

Natural neck of fairway between hill and stream restricts long driving.

TREES

Tee shot must hug stream or uphill approach will exceed 200 yards.

A good 3-shot hole for short hitter—wide driving area, but must decide whether to carry last crossing of stream with second shot.

#10 HIGHLANDS C.C. (ROSS).
431 YARDS   PAR 4.

Green opens for direct carry, but front-left bunker must be carried with pitch if pin is on left (upper) tier.

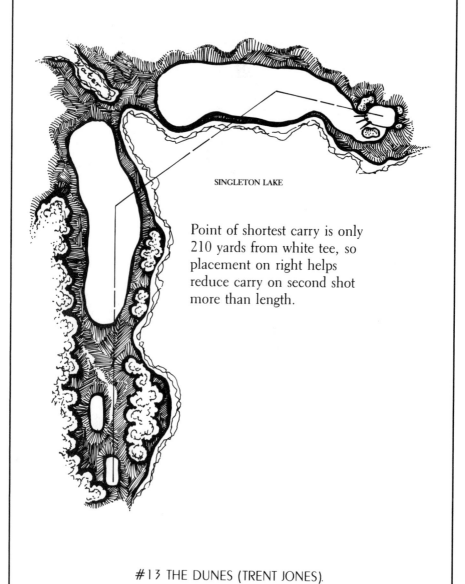

SINGLETON LAKE

Point of shortest carry is only 210 yards from white tee, so placement on right helps reduce carry on second shot more than length.

#13 THE DUNES (TRENT JONES).
576 YARDS   PAR 5.

164

hailed as the solution to the maintenance headaches posed by erodable and difficult-to-mow grass banks leading into water hazards. Still, I know that Pete Dye, who is primarily responsible for popularizing the use of bulkheads, was attracted to them because they established an architectural edge to hazards where the water level (and the edge of the shoreline) would fluctuate from season to season.

There are problems as well as advantages to the bulkheads, however. If a green is located at the edge of the wall, the abruptness of the edge makes it impossible to turn a greens mower around, leading to compaction of the soil near the wall. Bulkheads are also expensive to build and subject to deterioration over time, particularly in the case of railroad-tie bulkheads, which can no longer be treated with creosote or copper sulfate to slow the aging process. Finally, as with water hazards in general, the use of bulkheads has become so prevalent that they no longer have a sense of originality.

My personal dislike of bulkheads goes back to my primary objection to water hazards—they eliminate the recovery shot. The most exciting golf shots associated with water hazards are attempted recoveries from the very edge, such as Curtis Strange's gallant (but ultimately foolhardy) attempt to play out of Rae's Creek on the 67th hole of the Masters Tournament in 1985. Today, with a bulkhead in place to reduce erosion in the creek, Masters competitors have no choice but to accept a penalty stroke if their approaches are errant. And penalty strokes are simply not what golf is all about.

11

TREES
AND OTHER
OBSTACLES

*"A narrow plateau for a green, or a few hummocks in
front of one, will very likely cause just as much trouble
and amusement to a player as a gaping chasm stretching
right across the course."*
— HARRY S. COLT, *"Golf Architecture," from* The Book
of The Links, *Martin H. F. Sutton, ed., 1912.*

Though bunkers and water are the only situations defined as
hazards by the Rules of Golf, there are many other situations
"through the green" requiring the golfer to alter his normal
shot in some way, that can be used by the architect in setting
the strategy of the hole. These include: out-of-bounds, topography, mounds, grass bunkers, "chipping areas," trees, and
indigenous hazards. In this chapter I will attempt to summar-
ize the possibilities of each.

Out-of-bounds is governed by the most severe of golfing
penalties, stroke and distance, and for that reason is avoided by
architects to the greatest possible extent. If the boundary is a

physical one along the edge of a course, safety also demands that holes be placed so no person outside the boundary is unduly threatened; the club and even the architect can be found liable if an accident occurs. A common solution is to place the tee and green near the boundary, but to dogleg the fairway away from the fence line, planting trees along the perimeter for disguise and to discourage short-cuts.

When a course must be routed in corridors through a development of homes to be designated out-of-bounds, it is essential that the corridors be wide enough to allow considerable latitude for miss hits. A hole with development on both sides must have a corridor at least 300 feet in width, or conflicts will be frequent. When the corridor contains two parallel holes, some overlap is allowable because a stray shot to the middle does not endanger homeowners, but there must be a minimum 500 feet of width for the two holes.

Occasionally, but advisedly, an out-of-bounds hazard may be deliberately incorporated into the strategy of a golf hole. Several holes on the Old Course at St. Andrews are bordered by out-of-bounds. At the Road hole, the drive is famously across an out-of-bounds area and back onto the links, while the 16th tempts players to squeeze their tee shot between the Principal's Nose bunker and the boundary for the best angle to the green. But these holes would be unsafe were not the adjoining land part of the Eden Course, where other golfers know to be on the lookout.

An area within the course may sometimes be declared out-of-bounds to prevent danger, such as the practice area or an adjacent fairway that might be used to shortcut a dogleg hole, although the architect should try his utmost to find another solution. The Royal Liverpool club at Hoylake, England, is notorious for its internal out-of-bounds hazards, concocted to provide a measure of strategy on a flattish course poor in natural hazards. Today, hazards could be created easily through earthmoving; but the paralyzing effect of the "cops" at Royal Liverpool, particularly at the long par-3 7th hole, is fascinating to observe.

OUT OF BOUNDS

Plenty of space to bail out on right, but leaving a run-up through shallow valley with out-of-bounds right behind green. The further right you go, the tougher this shot becomes.

#7 ROYAL LIVERPOOL.
200 YARDS   PAR 3.

By contrast, the undulations of the ground are the most subtle of obstacles in golf, but provide some of the most interesting play. The British links are undulating to no end, requiring that most shots from the fairway be played from an uneven lie. They give the advantage to the player who knows how to adjust his stance or swing, or how to allow for the natural effect of the lie upon the flight of the ball.

The scale of undulations on the links ensures that a variety of stances will be encountered over a full round through random luck. On property of larger and gentler hills, the architect can add much interest to the course by locating holes so that the landing areas will include uphill, downhill, and sidehill slopes. If there is a great range of undulations available, he may design some of his holes to provide a flat lie to the golfer who places his shot in a specific portion of the fairway. A simple example is the par-4 15th hole at Winged Foot-West, where the professional has a choice between sacrificing length from the tee to assure a flat lie for the approach, or driving for a narrow corner of the fairway and risking the possibility of having to play his approach from a hanging lie. The same concept might be used on relatively flat terrain, by introducing some undulation in the fairway just at the length of a good drive, but just for a small portion of the total length of the hole.

The very best par-5 hole I have seen, the 8th at Crystal Downs, is another fine example of how ground contours can be used to full effect. This hole stands apart from most three-shot holes because of the importance of placing the second shot along a ridge on the right side of the fairway, if one is to have a fair stance for the third shot to a small green. The problem is compounded by the severe undulations in the landing area for the tee shot, making it most difficult to hit a long-iron or fairway-wood second shot with any confidence the ball will fly straight.

The other accepted method of using subtle contours to add interest to the course is on the approach to the green. This has

Narrow entrance to green
makes a tough second shot for
short drivers.

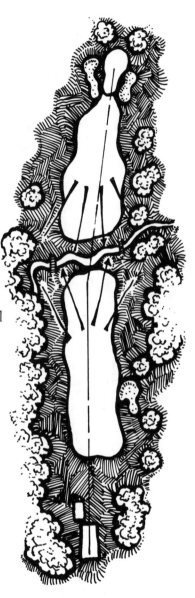

Landing area falls off down hill
to stream at 240 yards from
tee, forcing golfers to choose
between laying up or risking a
hanging lie for second shot.

#15 WINGED FOOT—WEST (TILLINGHAST).
417 YARDS   PAR 4.

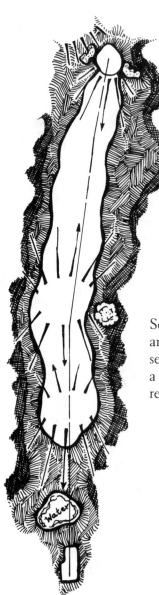

Small, elevated green a very tough target for long approaches.

Second-shot landing area falls sharply to left, leaving a much tougher stance for approach.

Severe undulations in landing area give difficult stances for second shot, sometimes making a fairway wood or long iron a reckless option.

#8 CRYSTAL DOWNS (MACKENZIE/MAXWELL).
550 YARDS   PAR 5.

been overlooked by the majority of American architects in the modern era. They either have visualized the approach as strictly an aerial attack on the green, or find it too difficult to include in the grading plan the sort of contours that create interest: low swells and gentle swales. But it is exactly contours such as these that make such courses as St. Andrews and Pinehurst No. 2 so outstanding.

A related feature found on some courses is the "chipping area," where part of the area around the green is mowed at fairway height to give the player the options of pitching, running, or putting from the apron back onto the green. The recent popularity of chipping areas is directly traceable to their use by Donald Ross at Pinehurst No. 2, although Augusta National and many British links have similarly maintained areas. One noteworthy example is Royal Dornoch, where steep banks at the sides of the plateau greens are shaved to fairway height. This allows a choice of recovery shots, but it also ensures that a ball failing to attain the green will run all the way back down the bank instead of being held up by long grass, magnifying approach-shot errors. By no coincidence, Dornoch was the boyhood home of Ross.

Chipping areas add considerable interest to short game play, especially where there are pronounced folds or undulations at the edge of the green. However, it is important that the chipping area be placed where it fits with the hole and where it can be naturally blended into the fairway: say, to the right of a green with a hazard at left. Some modern designs place chipping areas in isolated hollows where it is something of a fluke to find them, instead of in a location where the golfer might deliberately "hedge" on his approach.

"Grass bunkers," artificial depressions of rough grass rather than sand, are also popular on modern courses, although they do not have as noble an origin as many golfers believe. Nearly all grass bunkers found on vintage courses originally were sand bunkers, since grassed over to reduce maintenance costs. This economic benefit is worth consideration on municipal courses, or where sand is scarce and expensive to procure. However, sand is the traditional hazard of golf, and the average golfer will not easily be convinced that a course without sand could be a good one. [1]

Proponents of grass bunkers argue, and it is worth noting, that most good players are so proficient from sand that the grass bunker would possess more penal value as a hazard. But if the architect's object is to reward skill in recovery play, the sand bunker is the truer test; grass bunkers are vexing due to the uncertainty of how the ball will react when so much grass intervenes between clubface and ball.

Since the grass bunker is nothing more than an artificial depression of rough grass, it is difficult to see how it provides any more interest than rough itself. A variety of lies in the rough around the green, some above the level of the green as well as below, would be more interesting and look more natural than a simple series of depressions. For this reason, I believe the entire concept of the grass bunker is overrated.

Mounding, or artificial contouring, was a part of the earliest American courses out of necessity. Rocks encountered while plowing the fairways for seeding were stacked up in strategic locations, covered with dirt, and grassed over, creating the "chocolate drops" which add so much character to courses in New England. On contemporary courses, the power of modern construction equipment has given rise to mounding for visual purposes on a far larger scale. Yet it is the subtle and small-scale hazards that have the most pleasing effect: obviously artificial mounding identifiable from any distance detracts from the otherwise pristine landscape.

Sometimes, too, an obstacle many architects would destroy because it is not a traditional hazard can become the center-

---

[1]Royal Ashdown Forest Golf Club, England, features a fine course without bunkers, owing to its location in a Royal forest where artificial construction was strictly prohibited. But, it must also be said, the course could almost certainly be improved if a few strategically placed bunkers were allowed.

Out-of-bounds behind green.

Green perched atop 70-foot cliff, a short approach deflects back to right, more unpredictably with lower-trajectory second-shot approaches.

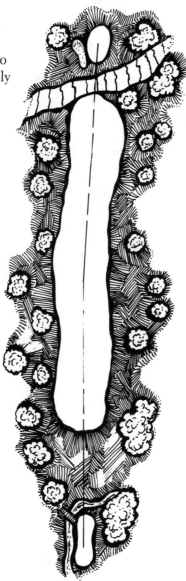

#16 DORNICK HILLS (MAXWELL).
PAR 5.

piece of a unique golf hole. The road and stationmaster's garden on the famed 17th at St. Andrews both fall into this category, and the maintenance barn at the 6th hole at Baltimore Country Club guards the dogleg in a similar fashion. Such hazards may be unusual, but they tie the golf course to the land and the community, and lend it an original and memorable quality.

On many modern courses I have seen rock outcroppings left in the field of play, raising the possibility that an errant shot may be cruelly deflected. This is a severe hazard, and the architect must be extremely careful that the exposed surface does not threaten a sudden and direct rebound at the golfer. But one cannot deny the natural appeal of such a hole as the 16th at Dornick Hills, Oklahoma, with its green perched atop a narrow ridge faced by a stone cliff, or the 13th at North Berwick, Scotland, with the green hidden in a hollow behind a low stone wall, the remnant of an earlier century.

VEGETATION AS A HAZARD

"Trees are a fluky and obnoxious form of hazard, but they afford rather good protection, and if a clump of these exists at such a spot it might well be considered justifiable to leave it standing."

—H. S. COLT, *Some Essays on Golf Course Architecture*, 1920.

Trees were not considered a particular advantage to have on a property in the early days of golf course design. Players objected to the inequitable nature of trees as a hazard, because a tree trunk can stymie one ball without affecting another just a couple of feet away. Most of all, trees were frowned upon because they were not found on the original British links.

Other vegetative hazards were accepted. Heather and gorse were an integral part of the links challenge, even though the dense nature of gorse made recovery impossible, the only place on the links where an unplayable situation was accepted as part of the game.

Today's architect is not as choosy; he uses what he has for vegetative hazards. Ferns, prairie grasses, and even desert can supply interesting substitutes for rough grass in the peripheral areas of play, as do the pine barrens of Pine Valley. The only requirement is that it be fairly possible to locate the ball in the midst of such a natural area and to get it back into play. This is often easier said than done. Many clients who say they aspire to the "unmaintained" look of Pine Valley have no idea just how much maintenance must be performed in such areas to prevent erosion of the sand and keep the shrubbery from becoming overgrown.

However, in most parts of the world, trees are the most common form of vegetative hazard. The architect is happy to find his property studded with specimen trees, for they add considerable local character to the golf course. But the wise architect is cautious when bringing trees into the play of his holes, because their three-dimensional presence has a greater impact on the errant golfer than any other hazard.

As living organisms, trees exert increasing influence over the golf hole where which they reside, and are as unpredictable as human beings. The only certainty is that if a tree is ideally suited to the strategy of a hole today, it will have too much influence in twenty years' time. And any hole designed around a single tree is doomed to obsolescence when the tree dies. The reliance upon one native species is particularly ill-advised, as any club once graced by American elms can testify.

Developers and club members also tend to become sentimentally attached to trees, regardless of their position on a proposed golf hole, and may refuse to cut down a particular tree. The same applies to existing courses where trees have grown unchecked for generations, or where small trees have been planted too close to the line of play by well-intentioned, but less than farsighted, beautification committees. Even where the original architect clearly did not intend for the strategy of a hole to include trees (as many old-time architects, including Colt, did not), the point is lost on members who have become accustomed to their presence.

No one wants to waste time and effort to remove a large tree if it is not in the way. But trees can be the bane of the average golfer, because their three-dimensional presence influences the trajectory of all shots passing by, and the Rules of Golf offer no relief. Anyone who has had an off day with the driver on a tight wooded course and found themselves ricocheting off tree trunks on their recovery shots can appreciate the point.

Yet if a clearing is comfortably wide for the average golfer, then trees along the margins may add shotmaking interest to the hole. For example, the player whose drive comes to rest along the very right edge of the clearing must usually play a fade for his second; and if he slices a bit further to the right, he may have to play a very low shot out from underneath the trees. In an age where shotmaking is seldom necessary, this is a very valuable feature.

Trees may also be used as a strategic hazard, where the tree is clearly healthy and as long as some latitude is given for the tree to grow without the hole changing considerably. A simple example is the 18th at Woodhall Spa, England. A huge oak tree on the right about 150 yards from the green means the tee shot must be kept to the left of the fairway to have a clear line to the green with the second shot, yet the green can still be reached after a wayward drive if the second shot is dramatically faded around the tree. This tree is perfectly located midway between the landing area and green. When trees are too close to the landing area, the difference between having a clear shot to the green or no shot at all rests more heavily on the matter of luck.

A variation on this theme is the 10th hole on my Black Forest course at Wilderness Valley, Michigan, featuring a "gate" of maples some 170 yards in front of the green. If the drive is not relatively straight, the second shot must curve

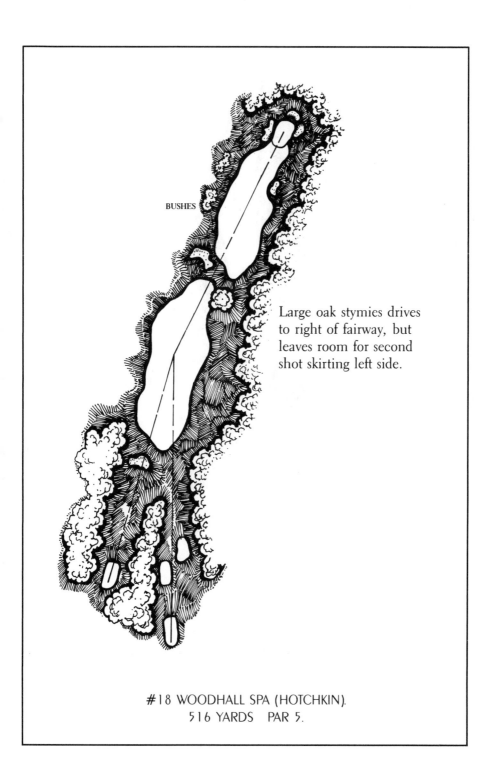

BUSHES

Large oak stymies drives to right of fairway, but leaves room for second shot skirting left side.

#18 WOODHALL SPA (HOTCHKIN).
516 YARDS   PAR 5.

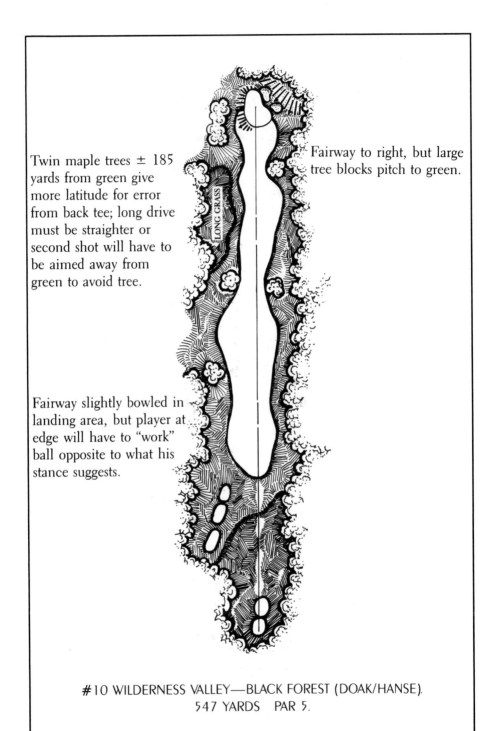

Twin maple trees ± 185 yards from green give more latitude for error from back tee; long drive must be straighter or second shot will have to be aimed away from green to avoid tree.

LONG GRASS

Fairway to right, but large tree blocks pitch to green.

Fairway slightly bowled in landing area, but player at edge will have to "work" ball opposite to what his stance suggests.

#10 WILDERNESS VALLEY—BLACK FOREST (DOAK/HANSE).
547 YARDS   PAR 5.

around one of the trees and back into the middle, usually from an opposing stance since the fairway runs down a narrow valley. The longer the drive, the more the trees will affect the angle at which the second shot can be played. This hole was inspired by the unusual "Faerie Dell" at Blairgowrie, where two trees on opposite sides of the entrance to the green encourage a running approach.

Another tree I think is particularly well-placed is on the 14th hole at Ganton, England, a very short par-4. This innocent-looking tree is actually just short of the landing area for a solid drive, so the golfer could choose to drive past it to take it out of play. But the length of the hole and the penalty for a hook—a large expanse of gorse bushes on the left—induce most players to hit an iron from the tee for safety. Then, if the iron shot is a poorly hit push-fade, the golfer may discover that his approach is stymied by the tree.

When clearing a course through trees, the good architect will be careful to cut a narrow path at first in order to save outstanding or specimen trees. Then he may consider whether to shift a tee or green site from the original location on the plan, skirting the best trees instead of removing them. Sometimes a single beautiful tree is found and the hole must be redesigned around it. A good example is the 14th at Oyster Bay, North Carolina, where a tremendous pine has been preserved in the driving zone and a wide clearing made around it, leaving the golfer the option of playing a low tee shot to either side of the tree or trying to carry the drive over its towering height. Remember that in bringing such a tree out into the open you are changing its habitat, and only sturdy trees not undermined during construction will survive the shock of the change to its microenvironment.

A tree in a doubtful position eventually has to be removed, and it is prudent to complete the task before it becomes a matter of club politics. If left to the last minute, such trees can provoke much bitterness between architect and client. A. W.

Gorse on left deters
aggressive drive.

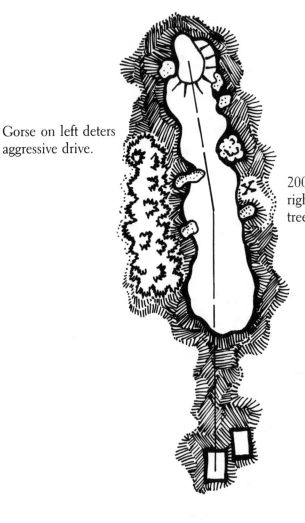

200-yard drive pushed to
right is stymied behind
tree.

#14 GANTON (COLT). 283 YARDS   PAR 4.

Tillinghast recognized this same problem in the 1920's when he wrote the following:

> "Often we find a large copse or a thick forest which must be penetrated. Those who grieve because of this necessity do not realize fully that opening up the fairway will not be a program of indiscriminate destruction but rather a painstaking effort to cut through in such a manner as to bring to view the best trees which long have been hidden away among unlovely companions."
> —A. W. TILLINGHAST, "Trees on the Golf Course," *Golf Illustrated*, 1928.

Sometimes the tree-cutter is forced to tell a white lie to achieve his objective. A violent windstorm or electrical storm, or a bulldozer operator who misunderstood his instructions, provides a convenient excuse to clandestinely remove one or two trees of contention.

A clearing should never be a straight corridor from tee to green; the wooded border should have a considerable variety of width if the clearing is to appear natural. It may be widened out in spots to highlight a fine tree situated back from the line of play, but it must always be wide enough that the weaker player can make a full swing at the ball without the numbing fear of losing his ball. A narrow chute of trees going back to the tee is a fine landscape feature, amplifying the satisfying crack of a well-hit drive. But the chute should always be wide enough not to inhibit a natural fade or draw, and the immediate precinct of the tee must allow sufficient light and air circulation for the health of the turf.

With respect to the final width of a clearing for a fairway, much depends on what is outside the wooded border. Where there are closely parallel fairways, the corridors may be quite narrow, since a miss hit may well find a good lie in the next fairway over; but on holes routed through dense forest, it is always better to err on the side of generosity. Claustrophobic clearings inhibit both the golfer's swing, the speed of play, and the vigorous growth of turf. A clearing of 120 feet in width through pines, frequently seen on small courses trying to get by with single-row irrigation, is simply too narrow; 150 to 180 feet is much better, narrowed in strategic spots by a specimen tree or bunker.

There should be a certain amount of "secondary" clearing in any wooded setting, where small trees and the understory are cut thirty feet back from the edge of the trees. This facilitates the finding of wayward shots at the edge of the woods and gives the golfer some opportunity to play his ball back into position.

The golf architect should be consulted as to an overall landscaping plan for any course. Too many new courses are created with the same "Scottish" look. Where the landscape has to be created from scratch, an ambitious tree-planting program might set the course apart from the crowd. If the same budget resources now commonly devoted to earthmoving were also applied to landscaping, I believe that greater visual effects could be achieved.

On the other hand, many existing courses have planted trees where they block a vista, or worse yet, a golf shot. Often such landscaping is done by a club "beautification committee," with an annual budget for new plantings. Without an overall plan reviewed by a golf architect, the job is frequently hashed. Committees should be warned against planting any tree within forty yards of the line to a hole, since such trees may influence the line of play and conflict with the strategy suggested by the other hazards.

The basic rules of landscape architecture which should be followed by club landscaping committees are as follows:

1. Plant trees in groups of three or more; odd numbers within groups are generally considered more pleasing to the eye.
2. Plant trees of several different species, to ensure that

future disease problems (such as Dutch elm disease) do not wipe out an entire planting. Stick to species native to the area.

3. Avoid formal arrangements of plants, such as rows of trees along a fairway. These look out of place in the naturalized landscape of golf, and the loss of a single tree destroys the form.

For the planting of golf courses, the following additional considerations apply:

4. Use primarily deciduous trees, unless evergreens dominate the site. Shrubs or evergreens which branch low to the ground block recovery shots, and should be reserved for use as safety screens or visual buffers at the boundary of the course.

5. Plant a few large specimen trees, instead of several smaller ones. Committees often make the mistake of planting small trees too close together, only to have to thin them out in a few years.

6. Avoid plantings which will excessively shade greens and tees, causing turf problems down the road. Also, avoid trees with shallow roots or litter problems, such as honey locust or willows, which will require extensive maintenance by the golf course superintendent.

7. Avoid planting trees at the inside corner of a dogleg hole, or near the landing area of the fairway. Such placement leaves the question of whether the second shot is blocked by the trees a matter of a couple of yards to one side or another, and therefore a matter of luck. When the trees are located between landing areas, on the contrary, they will affect the trajectory of the second shot in proportion to the error of the drive.

8. Avoid planting trees in the same patterns on each hole. They should add visual variety to the individual holes.

9. Do not plant shrubs as yardage markers at the edge of the fairway. These not only look unnatural, but are a nuisance when mowing the roughs.

12

THE PRACTICE FACILITY

"'Before Johnny went to Westward Ho! he came out for two or three days, but not to play a round. He took a few clubs under his arm and wandered out over the course. Selecting the most difficult shots, he played them until he felt satisfied. He played some holes backward because they are more difficult that way. He picked out some of the longest carries and played a few pitches to sloping greens. And then, packing his bag, he went off and won the British [Amateur] Championship for the eighth time.'"
—A description of the practice regimen of John Ball, from Robert Hunter, The Links, 1926.

The only truly perfect practice facility is an empty golf course, because only there is it possible to practice every possible stroke one might need to get the ball in the hole.

Unfortunately, there aren't many empty golf courses these days. The game has grown popular, to the frustration of those who have been its devotees for many years. We can't play anywhere without a tee time and the threat of a six-hour round, and we don't have the luxury of hitting a few extra balls wherever we choose. The practice facility, once the refuge of a few tortured souls, has become a matter of necessity to us all.

Yet the practice facilities on the majority of courses, if they have them at all, appear to exist entirely as an afterthought. The typical practice facility consists of nothing more than a small, bare teeing ground and a field surrounded by netting for a target area, often too short to permit the golfers to practice with their wooden clubs and therefore belying the popular term "driving range." This is true not only of our municipal courses, but of many of the finest clubs in the land. There are fine courses which cannot be considered as potential championship sites because they lack adequate practice facilities, and others suffice only because part of a secondary course can be commandeered for a proper practice ground.

The reason that practice facilities are so poorly arranged is that until a few years ago, neither the developer nor the golf architect placed a very high priority on them. Most golfers looked upon the driving range as a place visited a couple of times in the early spring to practice before the golf course was opened for the season, and possibly as a place to unlimber the muscles before an important Sunday game. Undoubtedly, the limited appeal of the existing facilities did little to inspire the golfers to spend more time there. The golf architect's primary task was to arrange for the best 18 holes possible, and the prime land around the clubhouse was dedicated to the starting and finishing holes, unless the club's founders made a good practice facility one of their first stated priorities.

Now that we have come to value the practice facility, it is time that we gave more thought to its full potential. At Forest Highlands in Arizona, the clubhouse grill is oriented not toward the first tee or the eighteenth green, where players parade past, but to the practice tee where members linger, offering the opportunity to socialize. At Desert Highlands, the most prized facility of all is the 18-hole putting course, with steep contours reminiscent of the Ladies' Putting Green at St. Andrews, though more lushly landscaped. And even at hallowed Augusta National, the most fun per acre is to be found on the 9-hole Par 3 course, where the Masters competitors tune up every Wednesday afternoon before the tournament proper gets underway.

The practice facility should give the golfer opportunity to practice as many as possible of the shots he will find out on the course. Instead of a small flat tee or a rubber mat to hit from, the practice tee should be as large as possible, and parts of it should be mowed to fairway height and gently contoured so the golfer may practice from different lies and stances. There should also be a good-sized area of bunker to give the accomplished player a chance to practice picking his iron shots cleanly from the sand.

In the area of the tee there should ideally be all sort of creature comforts so the golfer will feel at home. There should be a few trees to provide a shaded teeing area on hot, sunny days; Steve Wynn's Shadow Creek practice tee is divided by plant materials into intimate areas big enough for one foursome each. And in colder climates there might be an indoor/outdoor arrangement so that players can hit from a warm, heated area. An enterprising club professional might arrange some sort of video setup, to offer his members state-of-the-art lessons.

The target area of the range should be equally well thought out. Practice is wasted exercise if the golfer's mental process is not engaged, and golf courses rarely offer a chance to belt a full shot into a field with little care as to where it lands, as we do on most driving ranges. Since the golf course always provides a definite target—whether a fairway or a green—the range should provide targets that require the golfer to aim, align, and visualize shots. The range should be at least 275 to 300 yards in length, so golfers can practice their full drives. It should also be exceptionally well marked, to determine the true distance of each club, since players rely on the yardage book so much these days. On southern courses, a fairway or target greens could be outlined in winter on a flat surface through careful overseeding; otherwise, these will have to be created either by earthmoving during construction of the practice facility, or by mowing the range in definite patterns.

While the careful maintenance of a five- or ten-acre practice range might be considered an extravagance at first glance, superintendents should keep in mind that a properly conditioned practice facility amounts to a large sod nursery, from which damaged areas on the main course could be quickly patched. The superintendent should also consider what grass would be ideal for the much-abused practice tee. Golfers expect the same grass on practice tees as they find on their fairways, but for cool-climate practice tees the quickly reestablished perennial ryegrass would seem a more practical choice than the slower-healing bentgrass and bluegrass tees commonly found.

The best practice facility will also include a green for chipping and bunker practice and a large putting green. In the interest of safety there should be a good space between them so that no one will be endangered by shots skulled out of the practice bunker.

The practice putting green should be quite large, as it will receive even more traffic than the typical green on the golf course—twice as large as the average green would be a good rule of thumb. It is absolutely imperative that the practice green be constructed and maintained the same as any other green on the course; for most golfers the main purpose of practice is to get adjusted to the speed of the greens just before they go out to play. Ideally, comparable contours and slopes to those on the course will also be provided.

The "putting course" has caught on in the past couple of years: an exceptionally large and exaggerated green with 18 holes, designed to be played in a particular order for the return of a score. The earliest forerunner is the Ladies' Putting Green at St. Andrews, also known as the "Himalayas" for the unbelievable undulations it contains. The very interesting Putting Course at Desert Highlands, designed by Gary Panks, has popularized the form in America. A green of such dimensions requires a commitment of considerable additional expense, but at Desert Highlands it has proven a popular and less time-consuming diversion for members and their wives. At St. Andrews it can be observed that many youngsters are first introduced to the joys of the game during an evening outing on the Himalayas.

At a time when the game is becoming so popular that it is difficult to find room for beginners on the main course, the putting course and the complete practice facility are certainly steps in the right direction.

13

CONSTRUCTION

"Much will depend on the intelligent interpretation of the architect's wishes. The experience of a foreman trained to the work is absolutely essential, as the original plan is almost certain to need slight but significant modifications—all of them demanding an intuitive understanding of the method of Nature in fashioning the line of a hill, the curve of a hollow or the subtlety of a slope. This instinct for rhythm and character must be felt by the person, whoever he may be, on whom rests the responsibility of carrying out the work, and it alone will help him to redeem any form of construction from the effects of artificiality and hardness."

—WETHERED and SIMPSON,
The Architectural Side of Golf, 1929.

In the sixty years since Thomas, Mackenzie, and Simpson wrote about golf course design, by far the greatest advances made in the field have been in the realm of construction. With the advent of modern construction equipment, the ability of the architect to reconfigure the landscape has increased a hundredfold. Theoretically, we should be able to foresee all the best natural holes to be found on a property and integrate them with the best holes of our own imagination.

Sadly, though, the practice of modern golf architecture has lagged far behind this ideal: Our imaginations are hopelessly limited in comparison to the wonders of Nature, and architects are too busy with too many courses to attend to the details of each.

The construction of an 18-hole course is an enormous undertaking, requiring the preparation of 100 acres of ground and the expenditure of millions of dollars. But over the years far greater sums will be spent on the upkeep of the course. It is in the financial interest of all concerned to do the job right the first time, to ensure that the course does not have to be closed at a later date to correct construction mistakes. It is certainly not an undertaking for novices, and there are now many large firms specializing in such work.

The exorbitant budgets common to the work of many modern golf architects are often inflated beyond reason. Some expensive construction practices may be ideal but they are probably unnecessary and inevitably drive up the total price (and profit potential) of the job. The difference between a mediocre course and a good one is many times not so much a question of money, as of the dedication of time and attention to detail in the design.

Many successful projects are completed with the developer as his own general contractor, and the golf course superintendent is hired in advance to serve as construction foreman. Local contractors can be hired for subcontracts such as clearing or irrigation installation, but if the architect can supply bulldozer operators to do the shaping work, then the superintendent can oversee the finish grading, drainage, and grassing of the course. This scheme has three major advantages: The architect is comfortable working with shapers familiar with his style, the superintendent is likely to understand future problems because he has been involved in the construction from the ground up, and the elimination of a general contractor prevents arguments over where the job ends, or worse, cutting corners in construction to increase the profit margin.

No matter how the construction of the course is carried out, the objective remains the same: to construct features (i.e. greens, tees, bunkers) which will distinguish the golf course and to ensure that the course can be maintained in proper

playing condition for a price consistent with the expected return on the investment.

For those who wish to undertake the work of construction
themselves, it is important to have an overall understanding of
the process of building a golf course. The construction process
is not a series of steps, but of overlapping steps, performed on
each successive hole in the following order:

1. Permits and Engineering.
2. Design, including irrigation design and order of
   pumping station.
3. Clearing, often accomplished in two phases: a narrow clearing down the centerline, after which the
   hole may be shifted to avoid specimen trees before
   the final clearing limits are determined.
4. Grubbing, or removal of roots and ground cover.
5. Heavy earthmoving, beginning with construction
   of irrigation pond where necessary.
6. Shaping of features (greens, tees, bunkers, mounds,
   bulkhead construction, etc.).
7. Drainage installation, including tile under greens
   and bunkers.
8. Irrigation installation.
9. Final grading of all surfaces, including installation
   of greens mix.
10. Construction of cart paths.
11. Seeding and sodding.
12. Grow-in.

This procedure will be followed for each hole, yet the holes
are not built one at a time, and not necessarily in numerical
order. Typically, while the clearing work is in progress, heavy
earthmoving will begin on the first holes cleared. The most
efficient construction program maximizes the overlapping of
steps, but this can be accomplished only with an experienced
contractor and an architect whose design is clearly in mind.

Scheduling the construction process is of the utmost importance. Developers want to get started as soon as the money is in place, but starting at the wrong time can wind up adding to construction costs in the long run. The foundation of the schedule is the optimum date for planting the grasses in the given climate. Everything else is calculated around that date. Two items often forgotten by the schedule-maker deserve special attention. It may take a month or more to grass all 18 holes, so the target date for seeding must take this into account. Sufficient time should also be allowed for weather disturbances, particularly if the course is to be built on poorly drained soil.

By far the five most important elements in proper golf course construction are drainage, irrigation, the shaping of features, specification of grasses, and grow-in.

DRAINAGE

Drainage is essential to the health of the turf and its ability to withstand the traffic of concentrated play. If the ground is not sufficiently dry, mowing cannot be performed without physical damage to the turf, and a finely groomed playing surface will be impossible to achieve regardless of budget.

The most important component of drainage is correct surface drainage. Runoff should be directed away from features such as greens and bunkers where it might cause maintenance problems, and surfaces designed to shed water so it does not puddle in a low spot. Any surface with less than 2 percent pitch is likely to shed water too slowly. It must also be assured that in hilly country all the runoff from surrounding land is not concentrated into one valley of such high drainage flow that erosion becomes a recurring problem. It has been said by more than one architect that successful golf course design is simply a matter of making the drainage features pleasing to the eye.

Where a natural low spot occurs, or where one is created in

the design, subsurface drainage via catch basins and drain tile is relied upon to carry excess runoff to a nearby outlet such as an existing storage pond, a dry well, or a retention basin. Many modern courses created on flat terrain rely extensively upon tile systems: the fairway is contoured into hills and valleys, and a main tile drain runs underneath the fairway to collect the water from each low spot. However, there must ultimately be an outlet several feet lower than the existing grade, to accept the drainage once it has been collected beneath the depressions.

Subsurface drainage is also installed under the greens and bunkers and sometimes the tees, as detailed in the chapters concerning each feature, to ensure that playing conditions are constantly maintained.

One additional problem of drainage is that the golf course, and especially a development built around it, increases the amount of runoff created by a storm. To prevent erosion off the site caused by the increased flow, nearly all communities have strict storm water–management laws requiring that runoff from any new development project cannot affect neighboring property. The golf architect must often create ponds or other drainage retention structures at the low end of his course or throughout it, to collect runoff during a storm and to release it at the rate occurring naturally prior to construction. This involves the construction of low earth berms across valleys foreign to the design of the course, unless their presence is cleverly concealed by a feature of the course.

IRRIGATION

An irrigation system must be provided sufficient to sustain the turf during periods of drought. On courses in temperate climates this may require only a simple design consisting of a single irrigation line running down the middle of each fairway, with regularly spaced heads. But in hilly terrain or on a course of sophisticated design, proper irrigation design is essential to ensure that the course can be watered evenly without creating wet spots leading to damaged turf. In arid or subtropical climates there must be a system so thorough that every turfed area receives adequate coverage.

On modern courses, a proper irrigation system can cost as much as one-fourth of the total construction budget. Be that as it may, the investment is a sound one, because on well-drained land the irrigation system is the most important factor in maintaining proper conditions for play. Where a course requires extensive irrigation, it is wise to hire an irrigation designer specializing in the design and construction of golf course systems.

The most common irrigation designs supplied by sprinkler companies are often less than ideal. On northern courses, the most common design is a single row down the middle of the fairway. But while the biggest sprinkler heads currently in use on golf courses throw water 90 feet, they only irrigate 65–70 feet to either side effectively enough to maintain turf. This may be sufficient for an existing course in a temperate climate, but it is not wide enough to "grow in" both the fairway and rough in the landing area of a new course. The next step, the double-row system, can be even worse, because the two parallel lines of sprinklers must be located down the left-center and right-center of the fairway: To keep the edges of the fairways green the middle must be watered twice as heavily. This problem is compounded when the fairway runs down a valley; a drive right down the heart of the valley is likely to become plugged in the turf, while a drive along either edge will receive a hard bounce from the drier ground, and roll back into the fairway well beyond the straighter drive. And the golf carts will often run right down the middle, tearing up the wet turf. Suffice it to say, more complicated irrigation designs are often worth the extra expense.

Courses using a variety of different grasses for greens, fairways, and roughs must also have a carefully designed irrigation system, if each grass is to be watered according to its needs. The development of new grasses with low water requirements will be a wasted effort if the irrigation system does not permit enough control to efficiently distribute the water in these areas.

SHAPING

Certainly, no method of constructing the course can be considered unless the builders are able to do quality shaping work which reflects the ideals of the design. The detailing of the greens and bunkers is the cornerstone of the golf architect's art, and their appearance on the plans is unimportant compared to their appearance in three dimensions on the ground. It is crucial that the architect have a good working relationship with the shapers who will carry out his instructions.

On the other hand, too much of a good thing is also possible. A major failing in modern golf architecture is the imposition of an architect's style on the land, rather than interpreting the plan in light of the landscape. Large construction companies professing to "know just what the architect wants" are partly responsible, by bulldozing natural features into familiar forms before the architect has time to react. I don't think the British architect, Fred Hawtree, knew how close we were to fulfilling his prophecy:

> "We have tagged along behind the techniques of earth moving to the point where there is a danger of imposing a standard concept on every site by sheer technical skill."
> —FRED W. HAWTREE, *The Golf Course*, 1981.

GRASSING

The specification of different grasses for use on the golf course is the architect's last responsibility, but one not to be taken lightly, considering the sums of money that will be spent in the future to back up his selections.

It is wise in such matters to yield to the advice of a consultant familiar with the maintenance of golf courses in the given locality, or to the recommendations of the man chosen as superintendent of the new course, for he is the one who must ultimately make the plan work.

By the same token, it is generally unwise to attempt innovations in grassing the course, because chronic problems in course conditioning will distract the golfer from what the architect has tried to achieve through his design. The modern architect's tendency to specify the easiest grass to establish, because it creates a better image or because it takes the burden of responsibility off the architect, has been bad for the game due to the economic standards it sets. If golfers would slightly lower their expectations of fairway turf, then architects might explore new turfgrass options which offer savings in water and chemical use without fear of the plan backfiring in their faces.

While there are thousands of varieties of grasses in nature and hundreds in cultivation, there are just a few which will stand up to the rigors of traffic and maintenance common to the tees, fairways, and greens of golf courses. Fairways are mowed every day at heights from one-half to one inch, and greens as low as one-eighth of an inch for championship play. Foot traffic is heavily concentrated on the greens, and divots and ball marks must quickly heal themselves. Under such stresses any grass is weakened and subject to competition from weeds, pests and disease. Even the best grasses have their share of problems.

Outside the closely mown portions of the course, the architect has more latitude to experiment in his grassing plan. The use of grasses with contrasting textures, shades of green, or dormant colors can add tremendously to the visual definition of a course. In fact, on an open piece of ground, the use of tall sparse grasses in the rough may supply the only clear visual definition. Architect Pete Dye has been a leader in experimenting with different grasses, as he pointed out in an interview years ago:

> "'What brought Harbour Town to life, I think, was the contrast in the grasses. Until Harbour Town, there had never been a course in the Carolinas with different grasses. The contrast in grasses has as much to do with the beauty of a course as the bunkers, the water, the rough, the trees.'"
>
> —PETE DYE, from *Golf: The Passion and The Challenge*, by Mark Mulvoy, 1977.

The varying growth habits of grasses may add interest to shotmaking by providing unusual lies in the rough. And it may be possible to use wildflower mixes or ground covers in peripheral areas of play or immediately surrounding teeing grounds, though caution must be taken to ensure that they do not become too thick and weedy. Whatever choices are made, there must be adequate control of the irrigation system to ensure that the superintendent has a fighting chance to satisfy each grass type.

Architects should always be on the lookout to preserve native plant materials within the course, so long as they will not cause an excess of lost balls. Native plants, whether meadow grasses or heather or yucca, add mightily to the individual character of the property.

It is critical for architects to become familiar with the habits of these plants in the field, and to stay abreast of turf research developments by the USGA Green Section and by major universities. The choice of grasses is as important to the golf course as the choice of upholstery to the interior designer.

GROW-IN

The most overlooked expense of any golf course construction job is the grow-in period: the time between when the course is seeded and when it can be opened for play. This item is often entirely omitted from a construction budget, because it is not part of the contractor's responsibility or his contract price—an omission capable of bankrupting projects before they are completed. Depending on the location and the timely completion of construction, the grow-in process may take as little as three months or as long as eighteen. The developer can expect to spend more than the monthly average for maintaining the course during this period, without any income from golfers to offset the costs.

The usual construction method is not to plant any of the finished holes until the course is fairly well complete, but in certain situations this is unadvisable due to the potential for severe weather that might require finish grading to be re-done. In such situations, irrigation construction should ideally follow closely behind the shapers, so each hole could be planted as it was finished; but this is impractical when the irrigation contractor wants to complete his work without delay.

The other possibility is for large parts of the course to be sodded. This solution is very expensive in terms of up-front cost, but it may save money (and possibly environmental damage) if reconstruction work caused by severe weather can be avoided. Sodding also reduces the constant patching of eroded areas which adds so much time and expense to the grow-in process, and allows the course to be opened sooner, generating added revenue.

The most important construction fundamental of all, however, is that any worthwhile work of art takes time and effort in its creation. Advance planning is crucial for timely and cost-effective completion of the work, but nothing can substitute for attention to detail during the construction of a golf course.

14

MAINTENANCE— THE ARCHITECT'S PERSPECTIVE

"If a course needs to be in great condition to be played effectively, then the design strategy is flawed."

—Tom Watson

Many parallels can be drawn between golf architecture and the allied field of golf course maintenance. Golf was well established long before either came into existence; it was the popularity of the game which required architects to build more courses, and golf course superintendents[1] to prevent players from destroying them. Over time, each field has grown distant

---

[1] There are many terms for the person responsible for maintaining the golf course. In Britain the title has always been respectfully the greenkeeper, although some American professionals object to the term. In Australia the title is "curator," which I particularly like.

from the art of working with Nature, to become a very specialized science of its own.

Both professions have the disadvantage of appearing rather simple to the golfer, who does not hesitate to offer his advice on either subject. In the case of golf course maintenance, this has been particularly troublesome. Superintendents have little choice but to prepare their courses to the satisfaction of the members, even when such preparation may be detrimental to the health of the course or counter to the intended design. Golf architects must share the blame; they are asked by club committees to comment on maintenance issues, even though very few of them have a real education or direct experience in the field. The architect Tom Simpson was more honest when he wrote that "broadly speaking, the only thing which should be allowed to interfere with the green-keeper is the weather."

Nonetheless, the golf architect has a vested interest in maintenance, because as conditions change, so does the golfer's perception of the design. Perry Maxwell's severely rolling greens almost force the golfer to defy gravity at modern championship speeds. Donald Ross's bunkers 20 yards in front of the greens at Pinehurst No. 2, designed for the days before irrigation when you had to carry the ball just over them to stop on the front of the green after a bounce and roll, are today often erroneously identified as visual deceptions. And irrigation has changed the nature of C. B. Macdonald's National Golf Links of America, where the severe contours which once sent drives careening toward bunkers on the outskirts of the fairway can now hold the ball on their slopes, requiring precarious stances for the next shot.

The architect must be careful not to design features which are impossible to maintain, or are so costly that they undermine the economics of the project: His best-laid plans will go unappreciated when the maintenance is not up to standard.

The most troubling aspect of golf course maintenance over the last decade has been the steep rise in maintenance budgets. The increase stems from the expectations of club members for continual improvements to the course, and it is the job of the golf course superintendent to live up to their demands. There has been no one watching over the situation to play devil's advocate, and question the need for such "improvements."

Golf courses have always competed with one another for bragging rights as the best-conditioned course in the vicinity, but in the past few years that competition has escalated to the scale of an arms race—and so have the associated costs. The most affluent American clubs have attempted to stretch the limits of improved turf cultivars by maintaining their courses at championship standard for everyday play. Greens and fairways are mowed shorter than ever, with smaller equipment which increases labor costs. These practices are defended by the green committeeman and the superintendent as promoting healthier turf; but in fact the opposite is true, as short cutting heights can badly stress the turf.

The average golfer has little understanding of the science of golf course maintenance. The verdant green courses garnering praise as being "in great condition" are often living right on the edge of major turf loss. Healthy turf has deep roots, allowing it to pick up nutrients during periods of stress. The more the turf is irrigated and the lower the grass is cut, the shallower the root system becomes and the more the grass is subject to damage from pests or encroachment from poorer grasses or weeds. In order to keep the driest spots green, the superintendent must overwater the grass around them. Therefore, ironically, the turf is often at its healthiest when the golf course is starting to turn brown.

Golf course maintenance can be approached from two different perspectives—as a science or an art. Superintendents from the old school practice their art much like the general practitioner of medicine, emphasizing a lean and healthy turf through aeration and moderate irrigation, and raising mowing heights slightly to reduce stress during extremes of weather or traffic. A newer breed of superintendent maintains his course at a championship standard year-round, but is forced to use every chemical at his disposal (much like an intensive-care physician treating a critically ill patient), because such turf is very much living on the edge.

Adding to the problem has been the fact that American architects have recognized the trend in maintenance and taken it for granted, designing green sites reachable only with a high shot over sand or water—shots which can be played solely from a perfect lie. The fallacy of this design style is that even a perfect drive can wind up in a divot scrape, making the required approach impossible. If such approaches are called for on the majority of holes, then the developer (and ultimately the golfer) is committed to trying to maintain the fairways in perfect condition *no matter what it costs.*

Golf course developers and club members must understand that there is a Law of Diminishing Returns that operates in the field of golf course maintenance. There is no such thing as the *perfect* golf course as long as there are golfers to take divots. On the typical course in a year-round golfing climate one might spend $300,000 per year to get the turf 85% perfect, another $300,000 to improve it the next 10%, and *another* $300,000 to improve it only another 4% to near-perfect status. If the course is properly designed, the last $600,000 of expense will be a matter of choice rather than necessity.

From the architect's perspective, even if the owner is not concerned with costs, a course in perfect condition is an extravagance going against the nature of the game. For one thing, after the architect has striven to make his course fit naturally into the landscape, artificial maintenance practices such as stripe-mowing the fairways immediately look out of place, even silly, where long grasses in the roughs are intended to recall a "Scottish" look. The more uniformly maintained a course, the less chance there is for the golfer to show some emotional discipline and a full range of shotmaking by overcoming the occasional difficult lie. H. S. Colt recognized this as far back as 1912:

> "I well remember an argument upon this point which
> I had some little time back at Sunningdale. . . . when

someone came up to me and admired the state of the green, out of sheer contrariness I objected, and said that the lies were getting much too good. My friend would not agree on the ground that if a good shot had been made, the player was entitled to the best of everything. But surely this can be overdone, as what we want to do, amongst other things, is to extract the very best golf from a man, and nothing does this so much as difficult lies and difficult stances. . . . This is generally the weakness of inland courses, and where they have been ploughed up and sown with seed the surface has in the past been usually levelled at the same time, and a number of small interesting details removed."

—*The Book of The Links,*
Martin H.F. Sutton, editor, 1912.

I often wonder if one of the reasons for the ascendancy of European golfers during the last decade has been their years of practice on overseas courses. They have had to learn to adapt to poor playing conditions, as opposed to the top American players, who have been competing over immaculately groomed courses since their days in junior golf.

The golf course superintendent, like the architect, must understand the game well enough to know what is essential to his purpose and what is superficial. He need not be a low-handicap player, but he should know where his members are likely to hit the ball and concentrate on keeping those areas in proper shape. Above all, he must not equate the value of his job with the size of the maintenance budget. On the contrary, the most valuable superintendent is the one who can keep the course in good condition for the least expense.

THE BRITISH TRADITION

The superintendent with doubts about his priorities would be wise to study the British links as a guide to the essentials of the game. The approach to golf differs considerably between Britain and America. American courses are artificial to a large degree, and so it is only to be expected that a great deal of money must be spent to maintain the artificial status quo. One almost expects to encounter signs warning golfers to "keep off the grass"—and in fact one often must, when riding in a golf cart.

British links, by contrast, are almost ideal for the growth of turfgrass because they were planned with this feature uppermost in mind. Greens were located on the best natural swards of turf. Even in 1890, when Horace Hutchinson wrote that the huge 5th green at St. Andrews was "the finest green in all of golf," he was praising it for its uniform turf rather than its interesting contours. As the sport grew in popularity, the job of greenkeeper was invented for keeping the course in playable condition. But the standards of play had already been set at a much more modest level than here in America. British golfers do not expect the greens to be kept at a fast pace year-round, and have no desire to pay for that standard. Instead of setting tournaments at an arbitrary date, clubs schedule competitions to coincide with the ideal season for the grass, and hope that the weather does not interfere.

The British philosophy stresses the upkeep of the greens, where the condition of the turf has most effect on scoring, and the area to be manicured is small. The rest of the course is left largely to the devices of Nature, because it is simply too large an area to maintain affordably. The Rules of Golf make no distinction between "fairway" and "rough," because on the links the line of demarcation is fuzzy at best. Lies in British fairways can be quite poor, depending on the luck of the draw. However, the open approaches of the greens allow the low shot played from a poor lie a chance to find the green.

British golfers refuse to pay a ransom for the vanity of "pure stands of turf." As long as the playing surface gives them a majority of good lies and no more hardship than their opponent, they do not demand a uniform appearance and a pleasing shade of green, even on greens where mixed stands of grass can influence play.

I still remember vividly my first tour of the Old Course at St. Andrews with the greenkeeper, Walter Woods. The greens there, as on all the famous links, are a mixture of fescue, bentgrass, and annual meadow grass (*Poa annua*), considered by many American superintendents a weed to eradicate. Walter manages the course to favor fescue as much as possible, irrigating deeply but infrequently during periods of drought to keep the percentage of *Poa annua* under control. But he didn't want to eliminate the *Poa* entirely; it helps the greens to recover from the stress of traffic, and it thrives during periods of wet or cold when the fescue does not. The British putting green is not just a community of plants, but a multiracial community, with each species doing its part in certain times of the year.

When I asked him about the difference in texture between the three grasses, and whether it influenced the roll of the ball on putts, Walter replied:

> "Our goal for the Open Championship is to have a good stand of fescue in the immediate area where the hole will be cut on the greens. The year before a championship is to be held here, we transplant good fescue from the edges of the green into the championship pin-placement areas. But it really doesn't worry me too much. Over a long putt things tend to even out, and on a short putt a good player will see a patch of *Poa annua*, and allow for it."

I still marvel at the simplicity of his logic: A real golfer doesn't complain about the conditions; he allows for them.

It is hard to imagine the pampered American golfer ever relaxing his expectations, but three factors could turn the tide: economic, invention, and environmental. The economic reality of American golf is that at a time when the sport is enjoying a boom of mass popularity, the cost of playing the game is being priced out of the average family's reach. There are still some municipal courses where $10 green fees can be found, but most of these are banal designs not even a fanatical golfer could enjoy. The better courses are spending as much on maintenance as the country clubs do, and fee increases are the consequence. When less affluent golfers lose interest in (or, shamefully, access to) the game, a lot of the upscale courses built during the current golf boom will have to scale back their expenditures—if they can.

A more hopeful possibility is that modern technology will somehow reduce maintenance expenses while maintaining the standards of fair play. At the moment, the hopes of the golf community are pinned to turfgrass research; millions of dollars are being ploughed into the discovery and propagation of grass strains that require less water and fertility. But the bulk of maintenance costs (and water and fertilizer) are spent on the fairways and greens, and research will have little impact if it is confined to grasses for the roughs.

The golf establishment must also be alert to research in other fields that may prove important to course maintenance. The most widely discussed controversy of the past five years concerned square-grooved iron clubs: Did their efficiency overcome the penalty value of long rough, and should they be outlawed for undermining the importance of straight driving play? Not one authority stopped to consider that if the clubs perform as well out of one-inch rough as from the fairway, then their acceptance might drastically reduce the need for perfect fairway conditions and lower the cost of the game considerably.

The most important influence on the future of golf course maintenance will almost certainly be the growing environmental concerns of the nongolfing public. The political reality is that for the 90 to 95 percent of the public who are not golfers, the use of pesticides and fertilizers on a golf course carries absolutely no benefit,[2] so why should they be willing to tolerate any risk, actual or perceived?

---

[2]The Golf Course Superintendents' Association of America and the American Society of Golf Course Architects have both published materials aimed at showing the environmental benefits of golf courses to the public-at-large.

The facts are that more than 400,000,000 rounds of golf are played annually in the United States alone, and that no serious illnesses can be directly attributed to the use of chemicals on golf courses. Yet as long as potentially lethal chemicals are used on golf courses, no amount of research will eliminate the potential risk to the satisfaction of the nongolfer. The burden of proof will remain on the golf community if pesticides are to be reapproved for use and permits for building new golf courses are to be obtained.

The most important step the golf industry can take is to meet the problem head on, not through political lobbying but by researching the ultimate fate of pesticides and fertilizers after application. Where possible, significantly cutting back the use of pesticides and chemicals on golf courses is a prudent step. The golf industry's defense against public concern has been to assert that no changes are necessary, because of the unspoken assumption that the game will suffer if course-maintenance standards are scaled back. Yet, if golfers accepted somewhat lower standards for fairway turf, the chemically maintained area of the course could be decreased by as much as 90 percent. Reduced chemical use would not only curtail public apprehension, it would lower the cost of playing the game—and perhaps encourage a higher percentage of the population to become devotees of golf, who would be more sympathetic to the needs of the game.

Golf architects must start building green complexes that remain playable even if the standards for fairway turf are relaxed. In fact, as we have seen, this same design feature helps make the game more enjoyable for the average golfer.

Benefits cited include the preservation of wildlife habitats in the less-maintained portions of the property, the preservation of green space in urban areas, the cooling effect of turfgrass, and the impact of the game on the local economy. But all of these benefits would still remain, if chemicals were not applied and the turf was somewhat less uniform.

The sport of golf can and will survive more flexible standards of course maintenance; it might even become stronger. The vanity of eye-appealing green turf is all that has to be sacrificed.

15

REDESIGN
AND RESTORATION

*"As a matter of fact, the great majority of the once-noted
veteran courses have gone through reconstruction ere now,
or they have disappeared from the earth."*
— A. W. TILLINGHAST, "Reconstructing
the Course," Golf Illustrated, 1928.

All artists would like to believe that their work is immortal,
but the golf architect cannot be so naive. A golf course is not
canvas or stone, but a community of plants which takes on a
life of its own. It is impossible to leave the design alone; the
strategy of holes is bound up with growing things which have
to be actively maintained. Trees grow inexorably toward the
line of play, shading the grass and stealing moisture from the
roots. Mowing patterns change subtly, a fraction of an inch
with each pass. Grass grows down into the edges of bunkers,
changing the look of sand faces, and sand exploded from the
bunkers creates raised lips and new contours at the edge of the

green. If the design of a golf course is not actively preserved by a sympathetic superintendent, it will eventually reach the point where it has to be restored or updated.

There are three distinct approaches an architect may take towards the matter of redesign: restoration to the original form of the course, renovation of the design to update it for modern play, and outright redesign. However, a fourth approach, haphazard redesign by club green committees or a lack of attention to natural change, also has a profound impact, and often supplies the impetus for planned changes by an architect.

While architects attempt to allow for natural growth, they cannot predict the actions of club committees. The committee man wants to "leave the course better than he found it," but this phrase implies change, and change is not always for the better. The most common type of change on American courses is tree planting by club beautification committees. In parkland settings, such plantings can add to the beauty of a course if a few rules of landscape architecture are followed. But committees must also recognize that new plantings can detract from the native beauty of a property—blocking views and breaking up the sweep of open spaces, standing out as foreign to the landscape, or worst of all interfering with the strategy of a golf hole. Those in charge of landscaping should carefully read Chapter 11, and if possible consult with the original architect for guidelines on the proper placement of any new trees.

Many golf courses have suffered from deliberate changes made by green committee chairmen who try to "improve the shot values of a hole," usually by eliminating either a fairway hazard giving them particular trouble, or one they do not understand because it never comes into play for them. Such work becomes a problem when it is designed from too narrow a perspective, without considering the course as a whole or the full range of players. When viewed in the long term, such changes may amount to a game of "musical bunkers" between greens chairmen, at considerable expense to the members.

The wisest green chairman knows when to leave well enough alone. Any club lucky enough to play over a recognized classic course would be best served pondering its original genius, instead of how the course might be modified.

Golf architects, unfortunately, are also victims of the classic Greek hubris. Redesign work is lucrative business, and one does not get paid for advising a club to maintain the status quo. To prove themselves worthy as designers, golf architects often convince themselves that changes are necessary to a course, even though the benefits of their changes are strictly a matter of opinion. In some cases this can be compared to the vanity of plastic surgery; in others, it straddles the line of unnecessary surgery and malpractice.

RESTORATION

Few clubs wish to admit they have deliberately or by neglect allowed their courses to change for the worse, but through haphazard design changes and growth, such things frequently happen. When approached by a club to consider design changes to a course, an architect's first step should be to examine the history of the course since the original design, and to determine if lost features should be restored.

Because restoration should always be considered, a club should look for an architect who has an appreciation of the original designer's work, but beware the man claiming to be sympathetic to many different styles. While many modern architects profess to understand the genius of Donald Ross or Willie Park, most of their courses have been changed so thoroughly over the years it is impossible for the modern observer to say with certainty he understands their principles, because he has only observed their modified work. It is too easy to rationalize a major change on the grounds that the original architect might have done the same thing, if he had had the equipment we do today. Too many architects have sought to make their name by remodeling a fine course because they are unable to create one from scratch.

RENOVATION

The rationale for renovation or updating a course stems from ongoing improvements in the areas of course conditioning, equipment, and standards of play. Over time all golf courses become somewhat easier than their designers envisioned; only the best have stood the test of time without significant change.

Even this is disputable, as we can see from a quick comparison of scorecards from yesterday and today, borrowing some figures from Robert Hunter's book, *The Links*, published in 1926:

TABLE 1.
Scorecard comparisons.

Course	Yardage 1926	Yardage 1991
National Golf Links of America	6,163	6,745
Garden City Golf Club	6,417	6,840
Merion - East	6,515	6,482
Pine Valley	6,446	6,765
Oakmont	6,707	6,989
St. Andrews (Old Course)	6,572 (1934)	6,933
Muirfield	6,712 (1934)	6,966
Royal Troon	6,525 (1934)	7,067
Inverness	6,569	6,982
The Country Club, Brookline	6,350	7,010
Harbour Town	6,655 (1969)	6,900

TPC at Sawgrass		
(Stadium)	——	6,950
Muirfield Village	——	7,106
Kiawah Island (Ocean)	——	7,753

In the first three cases, the courses are now considered to be too short to host a major professional championship, even though The National and Garden City have been considerably lengthened. Pine Valley and Oakmont have maintained their reputations for difficulty, but only after finding another 300 yards of real estate. Even hallowed British championship links have been stretched out over time. Inverness and The Country Club have both undergone massive redesign, building a few completely new holes in order to remain in consideration as championship venues. Modern tournament courses are all much longer than anything which existed in 1926. Even Harbour Town, noteworthy in 1969 for its emphasis on accuracy instead of strength, has found an extra 250 yards in twenty years.

The point of these comparisons is not to suggest that all courses need to be 7,000 yards long. In fact, it is noteworthy that so few of the courses listed above have broken that figure even today. The essence of the matter is that most of our championship courses *have* changed over time, in this and in other less measurable ways. Despite the best efforts of the governing bodies to establish an Overall Distance Standard to keep golfers from hitting the ball farther, they certainly do, and courses have been changed in order to keep pace.

Unfortunately, courses most in need of improvement are often least likely to contemplate it, while clubs able to quickly come up with money for changes to the course are those least in need. Great courses have been spoiled, even ruined, by redesign efforts that introduced elements foreign to the character of the course, or by failing in an attempt to make great holes more difficult or more fair.

Many courses lose their unique character by striving to keep up with modern times. As long as good players continue to drive farther (no matter whether the increase is due to the ball itself, or golf clubs, or stronger players), older courses will continue to lose ground, and some do not have the real estate to make adjustments. Even where real estate is available, the job is often hashed by a misguided or confused green committee.

The most common mistake is the addition of length to a course simply to increase the total on the scorecard. Many clubs make the mistake of extending the short par-4 holes, but these were always intended to test finesse rather than length. It is the long par-4 and par-5 holes that have lost their luster for the good player now that the ball travels farther; these are the holes that need strengthening.

When there is no real estate available for more back tees, it is often proposed that the fairway hazards be moved farther downrange to restore driving difficulty to the course, but this is a gross oversimplification. Some holes, such as severe doglegs, resist any attempted changes. At others, fairway bunkers have been located in relation to the green or the topography of the landing area, and moving the bunkers will change the philosophy of the hole. It is wrong to assume that there is a "magic distance" from the tee where fairway bunkers should be placed to test the better player as it ignores the differences between individual golfers. The location of all bunkers at any one distance ensures that the design will become obsolete 30 years later when the "magic distance" has changed. If fairway bunkers are dispersed everywhere between 150 and 300 yards off the tee, there will be no need to move them later on.

The bottom line on renovation is that the game would be better served if we tinkered with playing equipment rather than our great courses. New standards for golf balls could be quickly and easily introduced, at far less expense than the renovation of a course, to preserve the genius of architects of the classic period. As for newer courses designed for the modern, longer hitter, there is always room available for additional forward tees.

REDESIGN

There are thousands of existing golf courses built without much thought to the artistic aspects of golf architecture. Many of these could be dramatically improved for the enjoyment of the members by an architect following the principles outlined in this book. In fact, some of the greatest courses in the world are products of thoughtful redesign, such as Muirfield, Augusta National, Oakland Hills - South, and Woking. If a course is truly uninteresting to the majority of members, then outright redesign should be considered.

There is also the possibility, as environmental regulations grow and the available land for development continues to shrink, that someday in the not-too-distant future we may have to rely on redesigning our existing facilities because there will be no place left to develop new courses.

While weaknesses in the existing course are usually cited as the underlying reason for redesign work, the real moving force is more often vanity than necessity. Successful clubs in urban areas have more money than they know what to do with, the result of high initiation fees set by the demand for membership. It is the nature of members to believe that such monies should be spent "improving" the course, rather than reducing their annual dues.

Unlike a new course, where regardless of the critical success of the finished project, 18 new holes have been created for the golfer's exercise, on the redesign project nothing new has been created. You start with 18 holes and wind up with 18, and the question of improvement is strictly a matter of opinion. Worse yet, there are certain to be members of the club who liked the old scheme better. About the only thing to be said with certainty is that any change to an original design deviates from the original architect's decision on the matter, and stands a great chance of working against the continuity of the design.

If a club is going to redesign its course, then it should be sure that the proposed changes will improve its strategic interest, instead of merely its appearance. The most universal mistake of redesign work is to rebuild the course by adopting the latest trends in golf architecture. This can take any number of forms, from cosmetic changes such as adding bulkheads around the edge of ponds and transforming sand-faced bunkers into grass-faced (or vice versa), to substantial alterations such as adding new tees or water hazards, planting trees, moving fairway bunkers, softening green contours, and eliminating blind holes.

Those who have read this book carefully should understand it is foolish to think the repositioning of a handful of tees or bunkers will turn a simple course into a great one. To effect real improvements, good property, a good routing for the course, and a well-designed set of green complexes are the three essential ingredients, just as in the design of a new course. In fact, the mature landscaping of an existing course can be utilized in a redesign project to make the refurbished course look better than a new one. But the transformation is no simple matter. Significant improvements can seldom be accomplished in the spare time of the maintenance crew.

APPENDIX

AUTHOR'S CHOICE

GOLF COURSES WORTH STUDY

GREENS CONTOURING

Augusta National GC, Augusta, Georgia. (Mackenzie/
    Bobby Jones, Maxwell, Trent Jones)
Ballybunion GC - Old Course, Co. Kerry, IRELAND.
    (Sutton, Simpson)
The Camargo Club, Cincinnati, Ohio. (Raynor)
Charlotte CC, Charlotte, North Carolina. (Ross, Trent
    Jones)
Commonwealth GC, South Oakleigh, Melbourne,
    AUSTRALIA. (Bennett, Lane/Morpeth/Morcom)
Crooked Stick GC, Carmel, Indiana. (Dye)

Crystal Downs CC, Frankfort, Michigan. (Mackenzie/
  Maxwell)
Detroit GC - North Course, Detroit, Michigan. (Ross)
Forsgate CC - East Course, Jamesburg, New Jersey. (Banks)
Garden City GC, Garden City, New York. (Emmet, Travis)
Harbour Town Golf Links, Hilton Head, South Carolina.
  (Dye/Nicklaus)
High Pointe GC, Williamsburg, Michigan. (Doak/Mead)
Hollywood GC, Deal, New Jersey. (Travis, Dick Wilson)
The Legends Golf Complex - Heathland Course, Myrtle
  Beach, South Carolina. (Doak)
Long Cove Club, Hilton Head, South Carolina. (Dye)
Merion GC - East Course, Ardmore, Pennsylvania. (Hugh
  Wilson, Flynn)
Morfontaine GC, Senlis, FRANCE. (Simpson)
National Golf Links of America, Southampton, New York.
  (Macdonald)
North Berwick GC - West Links, North Berwick, East
  Lothian, SCOTLAND.
North Shore CC, Glen Head, New York. (Banks)
Oakland Hills CC - South Course, Birmingham, Michigan.
  (Ross, Trent Jones)
Oakmont CC, Oakmont, Pennsylvania. (Fownes)
Paraparaumu Beach GC, Paraparaumu Beach, Wellington,
  NEW ZEALAND. (Whyte/Russell)
Peachtree GC, Atlanta, Georgia. (Robert Trent Jones/Bobby
  Jones)
Pebble Beach GL, Pebble Beach, California. (Neville/
  Grant)
Pine Valley GC, Clementon, New Jersey. (Crump/Colt)
Pinehurst CC - Number Two Course, Pinehurst, North
  Carolina. (Ross)
Prairie Dunes CC, Hutchinson, Kansas. (Maxwell)
Prestwick GC, Prestwick, Ayrshire, SCOTLAND. (Morris,
  Braid/Stutt)
Rockport CC, Rockport, Texas. (Coore)
Royal Dornoch GC, Dornoch, Sutherland, SCOTLAND.
  (Morris, Sutherland, Duncan)

Royal Melbourne GC - West Course, Black Rock, Victoria,
AUSTRALIA. (Mackenzie/Russell)
Royal Worlington & Newmarket GC, Mildenhall, Suffolk,
ENGLAND. (A. M. Ross, Colt)
Somerset Hills CC, Bernardsville, New Jersey. (Tillinghast)
St. Andrews - Old Course, St. Andrews, Fife,
SCOTLAND. (ancient)
Tournament Players Club at Sawgrass - Stadium Course,
Ponte Vedra Beach, Florida. (Dye)
Westhampton CC, Westhampton, New York. (Raynor,
Silva)
Winged Foot GC - East and West Courses, Mamaroneck,
New York. (Tillinghast)
Woking GC, Woking, Surrey, ENGLAND. (Dunn,
Low/Paton)
Yale University GC, New Haven, Connecticut.
(Macdonald/Raynor)

BUNKERING

Bel Air CC, Los Angeles, California. (Thomas/Neville,
Dick Wilson, Trent Jones)
Bethpage State Park - Black Course, Farmingdale, New
York. (Tillinghast)
Carnoustie GC - Champsionship Course, Carnoustie,
SCOTLAND. (Robertson, Morris, Braid, Wright)
Crystal Downs
Cypress Point Club, Pebble Beach, California. (Mackenzie)
Desert Highlands CC, Scottsdale, Arizona. (Nicklaus)
Forsgate - East
Ganton GC, Ganton, Scarborough, Yorkshire, ENGLAND.
(Vardon, Braid, Colt, Fowler, Hutchison, Cotton)
Garden City GC
Indianwood G & CC - Old Course, Lake Orion, Michigan.
(Reid/Connellan)
Kingston Heath GC, Cheltenham, Melbourne,
AUSTRALIA. (Soutar, Mackenzie/Morcom)

Los Angeles CC - North Course, Los Angeles, California.
     (Thomas)
Merion - East
Muirfield - Honourable Company of Edinburgh Golfers,
     Gullane, SCOTLAND. (Colt, Simpson)
Myopia Hunt Club, South Hamilton, Massachusetts.
     (Leeds)
National GC of Australia, Cape Schanck, Victoria,
     AUSTRALIA. (R. T. Jones, Jr.)
National GL of America
Oakland Hills - South
Oakmont
Pine Valley
Pinehurst - No. 2
Prairie Dunes
Prestwick
Riviera CC, Pacific Palisades, California. (Thomas)
Royal Ashdown Forest GC - Old Course, Forest Row, East
     Sussex, ENGLAND. (A. T. Scott)
Royal County Down GC, Newcastle, Co. Down,
     NORTHERN IRELAND. (Morris)
Royal Lytham & St. Annes GC, St. Annes-on-Sea,
     Lancashire, ENGLAND. (Lowe, Fowler, Colt,
     Pennink)
Royal Melbourne - East and West
Royal North Devon GC, Westward Ho!, Devon,
     ENGLAND. (ancient, Fowler)
Royal Troon GC - Old Course, Troon, Ayrshire,
     SCOTLAND. (Fernie, Braid et al.)
Royal West Norfolk GC, Brancaster, Norfolk, ENGLAND.
     (Hutchinson/Ingleby, Hutchinson)
San Francisco GC, San Francisco, California. (Tillinghast)
Seminole GC, North Palm Beach, Florida. (Ross, Dick
     Wilson)
St. Andrews - Old Course
St. George's Hill GC, Weybridge, Surrey, ENGLAND.
     (Colt)
Walton Heath GC - Old Course, Tadworth, Surrey,
     ENGLAND. (Fowler)

Wilderness Valley GC - Black Forest Course, Gaylord, Michigan. (Doak/Hanse)

Winged Foot - West

Woking

Woodhall Spa GC, Woodhall Spa, Lincolnshire, ENGLAND. (Hotchkin)

Yarra Yarra GC, Bentleigh East, Melbourne, AUSTRALIA. (Mackenzie/Russell)

ROUTING

The Addington GC, Croydon, Surrey, ENGLAND. (Abercromby)

Ballybunion - Old Course

Bel Air

Camargo

Casa de Campo - Teeth of the Dog, La Romana, DOMINICAN REPUBLIC. (Dye)

The Creek Club, Locust Valley, New York. (Raynor)

Cruden Bay G & CC, Cruden Bay, Aberdeenshire, SCOTLAND. (Simpson)

Crystal Downs

Cypress Point

Fishers Island Club, Fishers Island, New York. (Raynor)

Forest Highlands GC, Flagstaff, Arizona. (Morrish/ Weiskopf)

Gleneagles GC - King's Course, Auchterarder, Perthshire, SCOTLAND. (Braid)

Hamilton G&CC, Ancaster, Ontario, CANADA. (Colt)

High Pointe

Highlands Golf Links, Ingonish, Cape Breton, Nova Scotia, CANADA. (Thompson)

Inverness Club, Toledo, Ohio. (Ross, Fazio)

Lahinch GC - Old Course, Co. Clare, IRELAND. (Morris, Gibson, Mackenzie)

Linville GC, Linville, North Carolina. (Ross)

Long Cove

Machrihanish GC, Machrihanish, SCOTLAND. (Morris)

Maidstone Club, East Hampton, New York. (Park)

Merion GC - East and West Courses, Ardmore,
    Pennsylvania. (Hugh Wilson)
Muirfield
Nefyn & District GC, Morfa Nefyn, WALES. (?, Hawtree/
    Jiggens)
New South Wales GC, La Perouse, Sydney, AUSTRALIA.
    (Mackenzie)
North Berwick - West Course
Notts GC, Hollinwell, Kirkby-in-Ashfield, ENGLAND.
    (Park, Taylor, Williamson)
Ojai Valley Inn & CC, Ojai, California. (Thomas/Bell,
    Morrish)
Pasatiempo GC, Santa Cruz, California. (Mackenzie)
Pebble Beach
Pine Valley
Portmarnock GC, Portmarnock, Co. Dublin, IRELAND.
    (Ross/Pickeman, Hawtree)
Prairie Dunes
Prestwick
Royal Adelaide GC, Seaton, AUSTRALIA. (Soutar,
    Mackenzie, Thomson/Wolveridge)
Royal Ashdown Forest - Old
Royal County Down
Royal Dornoch
Royal Melbourne
Royal North Devon
Royal Portrush GC, Portrush, Co. Antrim, NORTHERN
    IRELAND. (Colt)
Royal St. George's GC, Sandwich, Kent, ENGLAND.
    (Purves, Mackenzie)
Royal West Norfolk
Royal Worlington & Newmarket
Rye Golf Club, Camber, East Sussex, ENGLAND. (Colt)
San Francisco GC
Seminole
Shinnecock Hills GC, Southampton, New York. (Flynn/
    Toomey/Dick Wilson)
Sleepy Hollow CC, Scarborough-on-Hudson, New York.
    (Macdonald, Tillinghast, Trent Jones)

Spyglass Hill GC, Pebble Beach, California. (R. T. Jones)
St. Enodoc GC, Rock, Wadebridge, Cornwall,
    ENGLAND. (Braid)
St. George's G&CC, Islington, Ontario, CANADA.
    (Thompson, Robinson)
Swinley Forest GC, Ascot, Berkshire, ENGLAND. (Colt)
The Country Club, Brookline, Massachusetts. (Campbell,
    Flynn, Rees Jones)
Uplands G&CC, Thornhill, Ontario, CANADA.
    (Thompson)
Weston G&CC, Toronto, Ontario, CANADA. (Park)

OTHER COURSES OF INTEREST

Black Diamond GC, Lecanto, Florida. (T. Fazio)
Blackwolf Run GC - River Course, Kohler, Wisconsin.
    (Dye)
Blairgowrie GC - Wee Course, Blairgowrie, Perthshire,
    SCOTLAND. (Braid/Stutt)
Chicago GC, Wheaton, Illinois. (Macdonald/Raynor)
Colonial CC, Fort Worth, Texas. (Bredemus, Maxwell,
    Cupp)
Dornick Hills CC, Ardmore, Oklahoma. (Maxwell)
The Dunes G & Beach Club, Myrtle Beach, South
    Carolina. (Trent Jones)
Ekwanok CC, Manchester, Vermont. (J. Dunn/Travis,
    Cornish)
Firethorn CC, Lincoln, Nebraska. (Dye)
Franklin Hills CC, Franklin, Michigan. (Ross)
Haagsche GC, Wassenar, NETHERLANDS. (Colt/
    Alison/Morrison)
Highlands CC, Highlands, North Carolina. (Ross)
La Cumbre G & CC, Santa Barbara, California. (Thomas/
    Bell)
Liphook GC, Liphook, Hampshire, ENGLAND. (Croome,
    Simpson)
Mid Ocean Club, Tucker's Town, BERMUDA.
    (Macdonald, Trent Jones)

The Olympic Club - Lake Course, San Francisco,
California. (Whiting/Watson et al.)
Oyster Bay Golf Links, Sunset Beach, North Carolina.
(Dan Maples)
Palmetto GC, Aiken, South Carolina. (Leeds, Mackenzie)
Pennard GC, Southgate, Swansea, WALES. (unknown)
PGA West GC - Jack Nicklaus Private Course, La Quinta,
California. (Nicklaus)
PGA West GC - Stadium Course, La Quinta, California.
(Dye)
The Philadelphia CC, Gladwyne, Pennsylvania. (Flynn)
Piping Rock Club, Locust Valley, New York. (Macdonald/
Raynor)
The Pit GC, Pinehurst, North Carolina. (Dan Maples)
Quaker Ridge GC, Scarsdale, New York. (Tillinghast)
Ridgewood GC, Ridgewood, New Jersey. (Tillinghast)
Riverdale GC - Dunes Course, Brighton, Colorado. (Dye/
Doak)
Rosapenna GC, Rosapenna, Co. Donegal, IRELAND.
(Morris, Colt)
Royal Cinque Ports GC, Deal, Kent, ENGLAND. (T.
Dunn, Campbell)
Royal Liverpool GC, Hoylake, Merseyside, ENGLAND.
(G. Morris/Chambers, Braid, Colt, Pennink)
Shadow Creek GC, North Las Vegas, Nevada. (T. Fazio/
Wynn)
Shoreacres, Lake Bluff, Illinois. (Raynor)
Links at Spanish Bay, Pebble Beach, California. (R. T.
Jones, Jr./Watson/Tatum)
Sunningdale GC - Old and New Courses, Ascot, Berkshire,
ENGLAND. (Park, Colt)
The Golf Club, New Albany, Ohio. (Dye)
Ventana Canyon GC - Mountain Course, Tucson, Arizona.
(T. Fazio)
Wade Hampton GC, Cashiers, North Carolina. (T. Fazio)
Waterwood National CC, Huntsville, Texas. (Dye/Coore)
Wawashkamo GC, Mackinac Island, Michigan. (Alex
Smith)

West Sussex GC, Pulborough, ENGLAND. (Hutchison/
    Campbell)
Whippoorwill CC, Armonk, New York. (Banks)
Whitinsville GC, Whitinsville, Massachusetts. (Ross)
Worplesdon GC, Woking, Surrey, ENGLAND.
    (Abercromby)

GLOSSARY OF
GOLF
ARCHITECTURAL
TERMS

Approach - The shot to the green, or, the area just in front of the green where the approach shot may land and bounce onto the green.

Bail-out area - A portion of fairway relatively unguarded by hazards, where the golfer may aim for safety instead of attacking the primary target area.

Bay - A distinct compartment of sand within a bunker.

Berm - An artificially constructed mound, usually of a long and narrow shape.

Blind hole - A hole where the golfer cannot establish a clear line of sight to his target on one or more shots because of intervening topography. Opinions vary as to whether a hole should be classified "blind" if the approaching golfer can see the flag, but not the surface of the green.

Burn (Scot.) - a narrow, winding stream, frequently found as a links hazard.

Cape - A grassy promontory projecting partway into a bunker, dividing it into sections or bays.

Championship course - Term implying suitability of a course to host a tournament. In some countries, championship courses are designated by golf associations, but in the United States it is simply a marketing catchphrase without meaning.

Chocolate drops - A series of small mounds covered by rough grass, frequently found on courses of the classic era. Often these were built to bury rocks and debris dug up during the construction process.

Contour mowing - The mowing of a fairway in curvilinear lines, usually designed to narrow the fairway in less frequently used stretches and thus lower the total acreage of intensely maintained turf.

Course rating - The average score a scratch golfer might be expected to shoot from a given set of tees, as determined by an official course rating committee. In the United States, course ratings are measured to the tenth of a stroke.

Crowned green - A green that is highest along its central spine, and drains to either side.

Dogleg - A hole requiring the drive to be played away from the direct line to the green because of intervening trees, rough or hazards.

Double green - A green serving two different holes, each with its own separate flag.

Driveable par-4 - A par-4 hole of between 250 and 325 yards, designed with an entrance to the green so that long drivers might be able to reach the green with their tee shots in certain conditions.

Elephant or buried elephant - A large mound or contour within the putting surface.

Entrance - Same as approach (q.v.).

Executive course - A course made up exclusively of par-3 and shortish par-4 holes, with a total par of 55–66. Also known as a precision course.

Gorse - A dense, prickly evergreen shrub commonly found on British links courses, from which recovery shots are usually impossible. The term is sometimes misused in America to describe any densely vegetated area.

Grading - The changing of the contours of the ground by mechanical means.

Grass bunker - A deliberately created depression of rough grass.

Green speed - The relative speed at which a ball rolls on the green, dependent upon the type of grass, height of cut, and firmness of the surface. Specified either in general terms (slow, medium, fast) or as measured by a Stimpmeter (q.v.).

Gutty - Type of golf ball commonly used between 1846 and c. 1900. Manufactured of gutta percha rubber, it was less resilient than the modern ball, traveling perhaps 80% as far on long shots as today's ball.

Haskell ball - Type of golf ball patented by Coburn Haskell c. 1900, the forerunner of the modern ball.

Heather - A low-growing flowering shrub or ground cover common to British links and inland courses, from which a shot may be played with some difficulty. The term is erroneously used in the United States as a synonym for long rough.

Lay-up - A shot deliberately played short of a hazard, where the lie would have otherwise allowed a longer shot to be played.

Links - A seaside golf course constructed on naturally sandy ground with undulations formed by wind and receding tides. The first golf courses in Britain were all links. Frequently the term is misused in America to describe a) any course, b) any seaside course, or c) a course which does not return to the clubhouse at the 9th hole (as many authentic British links do not).

Long hole - In Britain, any par-5 hole; or more commonly, any hole requiring an approach shot with a wood or long iron.

Par - The expected integral score of a scratch player on a given hole, allowing two putts per green. Determined almost exclusively on the basis of length, with some modifications for topography or elevation, but not for relative difficulty. Par-3 is any hole under 250 yards for men (200 for women), par-4 between 251 and 470 yards (201–400 yards for women); and par-5 over 471 yards for men (over 401 yards for women).

Par-3 Course - A course consisting exclusively of holes of 250 yards of less.

Pin placement - The actual location of the hole on a green, or, a distinct portion of the green where holes may be fairly placed.

Postage-stamp green - A very small green (roughly 4,000 square feet and under). The 126-yard eighth at Royal Troon, Scotland, is famously named "Postage Stamp."

Pot bunker - A fairly small and relatively deep bunker, named because of its appearance. Most bunkers on links courses are generally of the pot variety.

Precision course - See Executive course.

Punch bowl - A green located in a hollow, so a ball hitting at its edge will generally roll toward the middle. Frequently found on early courses, where the water-collecting properties of such a site helped keep a good stand of turf.

Redan - A hole modeled after the 193-yard 15th at North Berwick West Links, Scotland, that features a green set along a narrow ridge at approximately 45 degrees to the line of play, and falling to the rear of the diagonal, defended by a deep bunker along the front flank and others along the rear flank. The original Redan name is believed to be derived from a fortress of the Crimean War.

Redesign - To deliberately change the design of a hole or course.

Restoration - The redesign of a course with the intention of returning its holes to their original form and character.

Road hole - The par-4 17th hole at the Old Course at St. Andrews, Scotland, featuring a narrow, angled plateau green set between a pot bunker on the near side and a road (in play) along its rear flank.

Routing - The positioning and sequence of holes on the ground.

"Scottish-style" - Advertising buzzword linking a new course to the early links. No real definition of the term exists, so the term is used to describe all sorts of features, including many that have no basis in Scottish courses.

Short hole - A par-3 hole, or any hole usually requiring a short iron approach.

Shotmaking - The deliberate alteration of a shot's trajectory from a straight flight pattern.

Slope rating - A measure of the severity of a course, or its added difficulty for a handicap player as opposed to a scratch golfer, used to determine if a player should receive extra handicap strokes for a match. An average course has a Slope rating of 113; the most difficult are slightly over 150, meaning that the higher-handicap player should receive 150/113 times his usual handicap allowance.

Sod-wall bunker - A bunker whose face is made almost vertical by stacking strips of sod one atop the next. Common on links courses to stabilize an erodable bunker face.

Specimen tree - A tree with special visual impact on the landscape.

Stadium course - A course designed with mounds at the sides of the fairways to facilitate spectator viewing during tournament play. The term is trademarked by the PGA Tour in America for its Tournament Players Club facilities.

Stimpmeter - A device invented by Dr. Stimpson to measure green speed. A ball is rolled down a metal ramp from an exact height, and the green speed is measured by the distance the ball rolls on a flat portion of the green.

Texas wedge - The putter, when used to approach from off the green surface itself.

Untouchable - A par-5 hole even the longest hitters cannot reach in two shots.

USGA green - A putting green constructed in accordance with the recommended method of the United States Golf Association's Green Section. The method provides for sub-drainage under three concurrent layers of gravel, coarse sand, and a special sand/peat/soil mixture, to create a perched water table effect and keep moisture low in the root zone of the grass.

Wetland - A poorly drained area of land with a high water table or seasonal standing water, currently regulated by United States law and therefore must be played over or around within the golf course.

INDEX